PERIOD RAILWAY MODELLING

BUILDINGS

By Vivien Thompson

A Peco Publication

Published by Peco Publications & Publicity Ltd., Pecoway Station Road, Seaton, Devon EX12 2LU

Printed by Dawson & Goodall Ltd., The Mendip Press, Bath BA1 1EN
1971

© Vivien Thompson 1971
SBN 900586 37 0

East Grinstead High Level—April, 1968

The scene which inspired the idea for preserving ex-LBSCR stations in model form

Contents

	page
Introduction	
GENERAL HINTS & TIPS	1
BRICK BUILT STATIONS	
Eastbourne	3
Wokingham	8
Rotherfield & Mark Cross	10
Slinfold	12
Chichester	14
STONE BUILT STATIONS	
Knitsley	25
Saltaire	27
WOODEN BUILT STATIONS	
Fittleworth	28
Petworth	29
Bute Street	31
St. Albans	33
LOCO SHEDS & WATER TOWERS	
St. Leonards West Marina	34
Eastbourne	
Glyn Neath	36
Littlehampton	36
Radlett	40
GOODS SHEDS	
Littlehampton	41
Eastbourne	43
SIGNAL CABINS	
Littlehampton	44
Fittleworth	44
Eastbourne	45
Glyn Neath	46
Claygate	46
OTHER RAILWAY BUILDINGS	
Chichester	48
Pocklington	49
SCALE DRAWINGS	
Eastbourne	54
Wokingham	56
Slinfold	58
Chichester	60
Petworth	70
Fittleworth	72
St. Leonards, West Marina	73
Littlehampton	75
Pocklington	78

Introduction

My first railway building was a woeful affair, fashioned from two pieces of cardboard and some old brickpaper one Sunday afternoon. At the time I was not interested in this side of modelling and the construction showed this. I proceeded to buy several of the excellent cardboard kits on the market until one day it dawned on me that my layout looked like everyone else's.

Thereupon I bought John Ahern's *Miniature Building Construction* and studied it deeply. The result was that my first real scratchbuilt effort was a model of Winchester station, L.S.W.R., from a drawing in his book. This model was built from card willingly given by local shopkeepers, glued with Lepage's liquid glue, and embellished with brickpapers and poster paint. After this foray into prototypical modelling, I was hooked. This station formed Ken's terminus on our layout to which I added a model of the old signal cabin at Charing Cross (calculated from a photograph in C. Hamilton Ellis's book *British Trains of Yesteryear*), a goods shed approximating to Swanage, and a model of Windsor & Eton loco shed, L.S.W.R., the latter also from a drawing in Ahern's book. This collection was intended to give the layout a Southern Railway flavour.

At that stage I was more keen on modelling the L.N.E.R., so I delved around in old magazines until I found a drawing which could be adapted to fit Ipswich, G.E.R. I had to adapt because there was a dearth of L.N.E.R. drawings. Working from two photographs of Ipswich and a drawing in the *Model Railway Constructor* of Teddington, I constructed another cardboard model, making it as accurate as I could. This station was given two G.N.R. signal cabins, Dunmow, G.E.R. goods shed (from a drawing in a modelling book by the Rev. Edward Beal), and a large, unwieldy loco shed of M.R. origin: Coalville. This was chosen as again it was the only loco shed of which I could find a drawing.

I now felt that anything other than prototype accuracy in buildings would not pass. My last cardboard model was that of Eastbourne roundhouse. After that I decided to experiment with styrene sheet to see if I could improve the standard of my buildings. The ultimate if drastic aim has also been to make a model so robust that if it were flung across the room it would emerge intact.

Once Eastbourne was finished and the railway room was virtually too full to permit a further layout, I had to turn to something else. Coachbuilding was out: I was told we already had too many; wagons, also; and locos. That left buildings. The amount of L.B.S.C.R. stations being closed, obliterated, rebuilt or deteriorating was alarming. The frontispiece tells its own sad story and partially motivated my resolve: this was to preserve a small bit of the past by modelling one of each type of L.B.S.C.R. stations, purely as static (or display) models. I would concentrate on closed or rebuilt stations, as I felt these had more value.

I consulted my file of station photographs and drew up a preliminary list: Midhurst type—I had already modelled Rotherfield & Mark Cross to a drawing in *Model Railway News*; Slinfold; Bramley & Wonersh or Cranleigh, similar stations to those at Southwater, Barnham, etc; Chichester (rebuilt); Kemp Town (similar to St. Leonards, West Marina); Havant (rebuilt); Steyning; Petworth; Fittleworth (similar to Hampden Park); Baynards. Later I added recently closed stations at Rowfant, Grange Road (akin to Burgess Hill, Dormans, etc); Littlehampton (rebuilt); Barcombe Mills.

So far this project has not progressed very far as in between modelling these stations I have constructed various Midland, North Eastern and Great Western models.

General Hints and Tips

My first step in constructing a model is to make a 4 mm drawing. Most architectural plans are to $\frac{1}{4}''$ to $1'$ or $\frac{1}{8}''$ to $1'$ scale and conversion is (or should be) simple. I find that nearly all problems can be sorted out in making the drawing and it is well worth the time and effort as one can get to know a building intimately at this stage. I then persuade my husband's secretary to Xerox off two copies; I work from one of these so as not to mess up the original.

The tools I use are few: Swann-Morton craft knife and numbers 1 and 3 blades; a $2'$ steel rule, divided into eighths on one side and millimetres on the other; various grades of sandpaper; thin nose pliers; pincers; 2H pencils; indiarubber; compass; an old pair of dividers for scribing circles; an adjustable reading lamp for evening work; a large piece of glass donated by a plumber. All modelling is now done on a worktable fashioned from a piece of chipboard 4′ × 2′ × 1″ stuck with Evostik onto a baize-less cardtable. Other implements which are used more seldom are: hacksaw, household pins, breadknife, gas-stove, Wagner vocal scores for sticking under pressure, Swiss files, hand-drill and clothes-pegs. For heavier work, hammer, nails and screwdriver are obviously required and used.

Drawing instruments employed: bow compass, Pelikan Graphos pen and 16A nib, Indian ink, drawing linen or paper.

Styrene sheet: I purchase this in sheets 26″ × 16″ in thicknesses ranging from 10 thou to 80 thou. The main thickness used is 40 thou. As has been stated many times before, styrene sheet is durable, can be cut, sanded, drilled and moulded once the material is known. A sharp, half-through cut will ensure a clean break, the resultant ridge on one side is then cleared with a craft knife. Apart from 40 thou, the sizes I use most are: 10 thou—window frames, guttering, ridging, flashing and door panelling; 20 thou—doors, window frames, sills, ridging, platform facing, framing on wooden stations, chimneys, banisters, stairs and balustrades on signal cabins; 30 thou—roofs, interior partitions; 80 thou—bases for display models. I use Britfix 77 polystyrene cement. I have been advised many times by friends to buy a bottle of solvent and a brush, but I stubbornly still adhere to a tube. I find it easy to use, clean (remember the pin!), and, with a child about the house, safe. For bonding any material other than plastic, or indeed any plastic 77 cannot tackle, I employ Evostik, again in the tube size.

Another invaluable aid to modelling is a photographic library of however modest proportions. Even recourse to the original architectural drawing can prove fatal: a good photograph will show up whatever additions, razing or alterations to the drawing have been made. In the interests of an accurate building model this is just as important as in the case of a loco, coach or wagon. It is also advisable to have these photographs housed in an easily accessible place—this is wrung from the heart as one can spend hours searching for missing photographs (or, come to that, articles in magazines.)

The craft knife: No. 1 blade is used for cutting, anything from 10 to 80 thou, but the latter does blunt blades quickly and a hacksaw is recommended. The No. 3 blade I use for all scribing: bricks, stonework, platform edging, slates, tiles. These blades last for at least a year with constant usage, but unlike the No. 1 do not take kindly to breaking down bit by bit with sharp-nosed pliers to gain the last extra sharp part. I use two holders, one for No. 1 blade, the other for No. 3, to save wear on the fixing screw—and also because whichever one I wanted the other blade was always in!

I have included in this book descriptions of the construction of many railway buildings, but here lay out several ideas common to all.

Outside walls, floors, ceilings—40 thou styrene sheet. Any wall which has been scribed for bricks or stone must have an inner layer or it will warp. When these two layers are glued, they must be left under pressure for at least twelve hours for complete flatness and drying out. Being mean in the matter of false roofs, ceilings, middle floors, interior partitions even when they won't show in the finished model is false economy: rigidity, squareness and strength are important; nothing looks worse than a badly aligned building. Generally the yard and platform walls fit outside the ends; when the right-angled join is dry, the brickwork is carried over the (should be) invisible join to the courses on the sides to improve the appearance. Platforms are made from 40 thou, 20 thou is too thin as I discovered when I left Wokingham in moderate sunshine! Bricks or stonework on platform edges are scribed on before the platform is raised to its correct height. Any plinths are added *after* the building has been cemented to the platform, this then eschews any chance of ugly unprototypical gaps between building and base.

Painting: I use plastic enamel and railway paints by Humbrol, though I find these wasteful in that however carefully one seals a tin after use, the paint dries up completely within a fortnight. Experiments with poster paints have proved successful, especially for stucco and whitewashed walls, though not for small surfaces, and the paint must be applied thickly. Recently

2

I tried using emulsion paint for the brickwork at Chichester and this is first rate, will not rub off, stands 'weathering', does not reflect light much and is also very cheap. The finest paintbrush I wield is an 0, and for most painting buy ordinary brushes from the local sweet shop as plastic paints are hard on brushes which are soon denuded of bristles.

When planning the construction of a building, it is best to take into account which walls need the full scribing treatment and which will fit between ends. The inner layer is always 1 mm shorter at each end than the top one, the same applying to the ends, and this ensures a rigid, square joint. Chamfering at the corners has been suggested but I find this difficult to accomplish and believe the method I employ is stronger—it's impossible to break the join open again once the glue is set.

Now follow descriptions of various types of railway buildings. There is obviously a Brighton bent, but I have also included structures from other railways to prevent one-company monotony.

Brick-built stations

Eastbourne was my first essay in modelling with styrene sheet, my previous experience in this medium being the construction of several coaches and wagons. It would perhaps have been better to begin styrene architectural models with something less ambitious, fewer mistakes would have been made, but modelling would be pretty dull if one always did the right thing straight away. In the ensuing description of how the Eastbourne station model was achieved I will also comment on the errors I committed, trying to explain why various parts are not as good as they could have been, in the hope that it will encourage modellers teetering on the brink of "having a go" at scratchbuilding in this medium.

As may already be known, my only drawings of Eastbourne were those of the ground plan, any further dimensions were calculated from photographs and measured on one short visit to the station. Errors made in the working out of these dimensions will be visible to anyone knowing Eastbourne intimately, to the casual observer they will most likely go undiscovered, so I will confine comments on mistakes to the model itself.

Armed with the ground plan of the main station block, I drew out the complete block onto 20 thou, allowing for the width of the walls outside, and marking out the interior partitions. This was wrong for a start, 20 thou is nowhere strong enough for the floor of a model and later I paid for this by the two sides of the block slightly twisting out of alignment; a 40 thou floor would have prevented this. I still like to draw out the ground plan on a base, but

Eastbourne: Terminus Road elevation

3

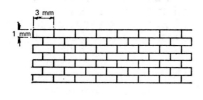

3 mm
1 mm

1

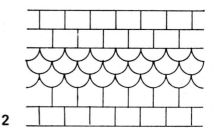

2

20 thou styrene sheet
Office punch
Take triangle out

Quarter with craft knife

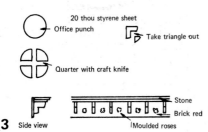

Stone
Brick red
3 Side view | Moulded roses

Pins stuck in a sandwich of 10 thou styrene sheet

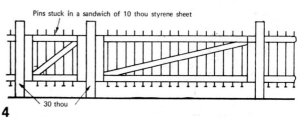

30 thou **4**

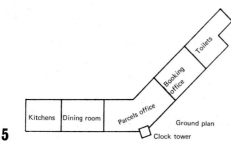

Toilets
Booking office
Kitchens | Dining room | Parcels office
Ground plan
Clock tower

5

now it is just that and not the floor of a model, the latter being put in place when the walls are assembled round it. The shape of the ground plan is shown in Fig. 5. I here acknowledge the excellent job Mr. C. J. Freezer made of the rough sketches I sent to accompany the original Eastbourne articles and which I am again using.

The first elevation built was that fronting onto Terminus Road. In the period I model (*c.* 1909) this part of the station was devoted to a large dining room and the kitchens; this elegant frontage has been displaced by a row of shops. This wing was 400 mm long and so was built in three pieces: kitchens, dining room (which was set forward 4 mm) and the parcels office. An overlap was left on each section for locating onto its neighbour. I then made my second mistake: this was using 30 thou for the sides. This seemed the obvious thickness at the time, but I have since realised that both for scale accuracy and

strength, 40 thou is correct. All buildings have been constructed of this thickness since. It was at this stage that I started my first scribing marathon; I still use the method I evolved here, despite the marketing of an already embossed brick styrene sheet. If one has the time and patience, I still think the do it yourself way best. Naturally the saving of time with the ready-made product is fine, but what about window apertures with brick variations—or arches— or any of the hundred and one differences which buildings sport?

I learned this scribing technique pretty thoroughly during the million-odd bricks produced at Eastbourne. The basic method is this: all horizontal courses are marked out at 1 mm intervals (omitting any masked by plinths, etc, that is a waste of time) and with a Swann-Morton no. 3 blade, the courses are scribed. When all these are completed, the vertical divisions are marked out every 1½ mm but the cuts made every 3 mm on each row, each succeeding row being 1½ mm indented, Fig. 1. What I did not do at Eastbourne and subsequently devised was to clean out every cut with the curved back of the blade. The Eastbourne courses are ridged, those on later buildings are slightly set in as on a real house.

On the first section I erred in sticking the two layers of 30 thou together first, drying them under pressure overnight with the aid of my "Ring" scores and *then* doing the scribing. Needless to say this had the effect of not only making the task twice as difficult but also the two layers showed a tendency to warp. Lesson learned: scribe top layer, then glue it to second layer and leave overnight under pressure. Another improvement which came from this first section was to cut the second layer 1 mm shorter at each end so that it would "key" into a similar arrangement on the other sides which meet at right angles. The first right angled join I made on the left end of this elevation was with both layers the same length and this is not as satisfactory as the later method adopted.

Eastbourne boasts two types of window and care was exercised to locate the correct one in each case, Fig. 6. Window frames were cut with a sharp no. 1 blade from 10 thou, painted buff, the excess paint being scraped off the back when dry, and then stuck in place behind the aperture. 10 thou glazing was added when the frames were dry. Door transoms were made in the same way, the doors themselves being tailored to each location and modelled either open or shut as seemed suitable.

When completed, the Terminus Road wing and the end wall of the kitchen were glued to the prepared floor. The finicky parts were then added: copings, cornices, modillons and other ornamentations. Fig. 3 shows how the modillons under the cornices were made. The balustrade above the dining room was built by forming a criss-cross pattern of 20 thou × 2 mm strips in the oblong openings. This is shown in the

Terminus Road roof—prototype

Terminus Road roof—model

two photographs, one of the prototype, the other of the model. The decorative balls were fashioned from beads and household pins.

The platform elevation walls were constructed in the same way: I had no photographs of this side, so the window types had to be conjectured. Next came the lantern wing, linked to the dining room section by the short wall behind the clock tower. The join under the clock tower was chamfered and given plenty of glue, the excess being cleaned off when thoroughly dry. Now partitions were added as shown on the ground plan and the booking hall modelled (this hall was the present-day refreshment room.) The inside of all

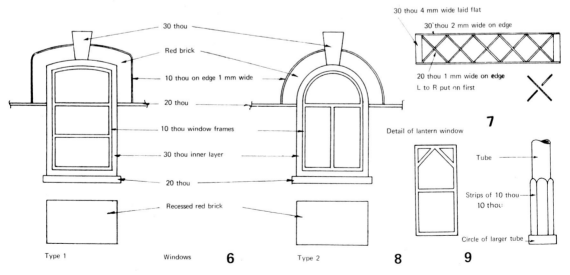

Type 1   Windows   **6**   Type 2   **8**   **9**

30 thou
Red brick
10 thou on edge 1 mm wide
20 thou
10 thou window frames
30 thou inner layer
20 thou
Recessed red brick

30 thou 4 mm wide laid flat
30 thou 2 mm wide on edge
20 thou 1 mm wide on edge
L to R put on first
7

Detail of lantern window

Tube
Strips of 10 thou
10 thou
Circle of larger tube

buildings, except for the booking hall which was painted dark brown, was treated to a coat of pale green paint. Once a flat roof had been put over the entire block, I realised I could have saved myself the trouble of either modelling the interior of the booking hall or painting any of the inside !

The brickwork was painted a rather too yellow shade with Humbrol colours; the fancy parts round windows and doors and under cornices were painted dark red. Modillons, cornices, window sills, keystones and surrounds, copings and balustrading were light grey.

Roofs were next on the agenda. The easier ones were 30 thou, a second layer being used on large sections. Fig. 2 shows the alternating rows of tiles. The rectangular slates were scribed as already explained for bricks, their size being 9 mm × 3 mm; the round tiles were indented with a 5 mm diameter leather punch. Ridging and flashing were 10 thou of suitable width. The most difficult roof was that behind the clock tower. Templates were first cut from card to save styrene wastage and when they were correct and fitted together properly, the requisite pieces were cut from 30 thou and scribed for slates. When the roof under the lantern had dried, the lantern itself was made from 20 thou; the ornate window frames were cut very carefully from 10 thou, all in one piece. The 20 thou was painted umber; the 10 thou buff. The two layers were stuck together when dry, 10 thou

glazing added, and then the four sides formed a box round a floor and flat roof. This box located into the aperture left by the lower roof. When dry, the top roof was added with a 30 thou flat crown. The coping on this roof was cut from a plastic traycloth and secured with Evostik; a pin being added in each corner. Guttering round the lantern roofs and clocktower was made from rubber protective handles on a Pyrex casserole and stuck in position with Evostik.

Eastbourne's clocktower was the most complicated and ornate part of the model. When built, it slotted over the raised parapet and was secured with plenty of glue. The semi-circular part under the bulk of the tower was formed from layers of 30 thou and Plasticine and painted grey when dry. The photographs show the intricacies of this tower better than words.

All the completed roofs were painted dark grey, with dull silver ridging and flashing; all guttering is umber.

It took me a whole morning to decide how to model the bulbous roof over the dining room. I built a shell of 10 thou shaped like a football bladder, convex and concave. This bladder was stuck to the flat roof and when dry was covered with about 16,000 tiles of 10 thou produced from an office punch. This long job was done in stages to prevent the whole structure collapsing into a gooey mess of melted styrene sheet. When completed it was topped with a square of 30 thou

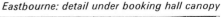

Eastbourne: detail under booking hall canopy

surmounted by an ornament from an old necklace and a flagpole from an Airfix ship kit.

Chimneys were built up from 30 thou sheet, scribed for bricks; the cowls were also 30 thou and the mouldings 20 thou. I learned another lesson here: if a chimney is to be sited in an awkward position, paint it before placing it there! Suffice to say that in position those chimneys were hell to paint . . .

The detailing of the concourse came next, an enjoyable job. The Brighton-type clock was made from layers of 30 thou, painted umber and the face added. It stands over the ex-booking hall entrance. I purchased two identical sheets of MRAS advertisements, measured each and built individual boards from 20 thou, allowing 1 mm extra all round. These boards were painted umber, the posters affixed when the paint was dry, and glued in position. Timetables were treated the same, using the Merco sheet. Finally the square-section drainpipes were made from 30 thou.

This having completed the main block, the subsidiary building which housed porters', lamp, inspectors' and coal rooms, etc., was built in the same manner. The windows were of more usual rectangular design. The fourth wall of this building was formed by the high wall, which was the same height as those on the main block, to carry the overall glazed roof. This roof was built up of 20 thou struts, the three spans having to be fitted carefully into the irregular shape of the main buildings. Once the glazing was in position, the clerestory section was cemented on, being made from 30 thou. The roof framework and clerestory sides were painted buff, the roofs of the latter sections being dark grey.

The girder which stretched from the main buildings to the opposite side across the platform ends was made of 30 thou, with a criss-cross overlay of 10 thou on each side. When this was dry, the two buildings were joined by this girder and left to stick overnight. I next built the two long girders which ran from the main girder to the rear of the dining room block and located onto the parapet. I first drew out the girders full size on paper and then stuck styrene strips to this plan. They were easily sliced off afterwards with a razor blade. The top and bottom members were 30 thou strips,

held at regular intervals with strips 30 thou × 4 mm set vertically. The criss-cross members were of 20 thou, cut out previously in great quantity so as to make the actual construction continuous, Fig. 7. These two girders were left for a few days to dry properly and then were glued into position. The painting was worse than the building! The seven supporting columns came from plastic tubing; each was ornamented at top and bottom, Fig. 9. When the columns were dry, the entire roof was stuck in place. The model was then put in position on the prepared platforms—and the whole of the Terminus Road frontage was so close to the wall it hardly showed! I think at this stage I should have stuck the model down to the cardboard base with Evostik, but I did not like to commit it irrevocably and so let it stand freely, glueing down only the columns as they showed a determined tendency to "wave in the breeze". Leaving the buildings unglued has paid off recently when the station was removed for alterations and needed only the columns slicing from the base and the two long platform canopies severing from the actual station. It has since been Evostik-ed to the base.

Before proceeding with more construction work, I detailed the concourse under the overall roof. Merit station seats (painted umber), luggage and trolleys, Airfix passengers and station staff, etc. were stuck down. The W. H. Smith bookstall, which in those days was situated along the left hand wall of the station, was built from various thicknesses of styrene sheet, covered in cut-up newspapers and periodicals. I had purchased a fine photograph of the concourse from Lens of Sutton and this enabled me to model the characteristic Excess Luggage Office, platform gates and fencing, Fig. 4. The Brighton-type hanging lamps were built from Airfix station lamps, a circle of 10 thou punched in the centre, a pin burned into the top and the pin-head affixed to the girder with Evostik.

The booking hall canopy was next built. There are ten sections and these were cut from 10 thou, as were the front and rear triangular pieces. A very sharp no. 1 blade was necessary for this fiddly work. Each section was glazed with 10 thou and then stuck to a base of girders (made as already explained) and the valances. The columns came from an Airfix canopy kit, with added ornamental bases and brackets of 20 thou.

Eastbourne: elevations to concourse

All of this was painted buff (except for the glazing!) and the columns were umber.

The same method was employed in the long canopy over the cab road between platforms 1 and 2, except that the apex of the triangular sections was at the base, butting onto the 30 thou sides which were overlaid at regular intervals with 10 thou strips. The vertical section below the roof is a continuous girder overlaid with strips of 20 thou, much the same as vents on meat vans, etc. Nineteen girders run at right angles to the long girders and columns are located below every other one, knitting needles of the correct diameter being used here fixed with Evostik as the styrene glue would not "take" on them. All the valances on the station were constructed from 30 thou, the vertical planks being scribed on and the sawtooth section cut with a shortened no. 1 blade. This scribing produces a decided upward curve on the valances and they have to be gently straightened again before sticking in place. Overlays are 10 thou strip. The long canopy over platforms 3 and 4 consisted merely of a flat roof of 30 thou, with 20 thou strips at regular intervals; valancing; and I-shaped girders, made from 30 thou, to support the structure. The two short canopies between the concourse and the main canopies are built in similar fashion, the columns being knitting needles suitably embellished.

As well as the drawings which have already appeared in *Railway Modeller*, I have included several detail shots of the Terminus Road frontage and also of the booking hall entrance before the canopy was secured in position, as views of these

sections, due to their masking when on the layout, have not been published before.

Wokingham is an S.E.C.R. station on the Reading-Redhill line deep in L.S.W.R. territory. Though the latter had running powers only and, so far as I know, had no hand in building this station, it does bear an architectural resemblance to several found on the L.S.W.R. system; as if to dispute this, the more ornate S.E.C.R. stations at Wateringbury and Aylesford on the Maidstone East line have a family likeness to Wokingham.

The model is of the up side buildings and platform only, mounted on a piece of parana pine $5' \times 9'' \times \frac{5}{8}''$. This was the first station model in which I used 40 thou styrene sheet in two layers for the sides, having as already stated learned from Eastbourne that 30 thou is not strong enough. Construction took a long time as I had no drawings other than the 40' to 1" track plan to work from and had to calculate all elevations from photographs. I have since been told I did not get the pitch of the roof right! I would stress that the drawings of Wokingham included here are worked out from my own photographs and a few measurements taken by myself and are therefore not claimed as accurate.

The first parts to be built were the platform and yard walls of the stationmaster's house; these were four layers of 40 thou, the top layer scribed for bricks right up to the point. Window frames were made from two layers of 10 thou, the inner layer including horizontal and vertical bars which were left white, and the frames locate behind the top layer. The side walls of this section were made next, both being two layers of 40 thou; that at the Reading end which formed the support for the adjacent roof is left mercifully blank of scribing; the London end side is scribed only where it will show above and between the many small buildings at this end. The two dormer walls needed some care, partially to get the actual dormers correct and also because the section at the Reading end (booking hall and entrance) stands 2 mm back from the adjoining part. Dormers were four layers of 40 thou, those facing the yard scribed for bricks, those on the platform side left blank as the walls above the canopy have been plastered. This similarly applies to the end wall on this section. The window frames again locate

Wokingham: detail of roofs near bridge on prototype

behind the top layer on the dormers and are of two layers.

The remainder of the building was made in the same manner. Copings on the pointed walls and dormers were of two thicknesses: 40 thou for the lower, 80 thou scribed every 3 mm for the top; it was necessary to chamfer the ends to meet at the required angle.

Roofs were 30 thou, scribed for slates, the first to be made being that over the stationmaster's house which located onto ribs behind the pointed walls, then working roof by roof towards the Reading end; that on the Ladies' is flat and made from 40 thou stuck below parapet as shown by dotted lines on the drawing. Chimneys proved the biggest headache and were built up, in all their odd shapes, from 40 thou, with 30 thou tops to each section. Pots are biro tubing or in the case of hexagonal shape made from pieces of 10 thou. Reference to the drawings included will show how each group stands.

The completed buildings were stuck to a 20 thou base—another of my mistakes as it warped alarmingly when left near a window, necessitating platform repairs. This base also formed the up platform which was raised to correct height on 40 thou

formers, ramps included. Platform facing was 20 thou, scribed for bricks and then cemented in front of the formers. The various ancillary buildings were added to the platform: their construction should be clear from the dimensioned porters' room; remaining building is a brick-built Gents'. Platform canopy was an L-shaped piece of 40 thou cut to fit the various corners, the valancing being 30 thou scribed for vertical planking; the "rosettes" are heads from household pins burned in and the excess cut off. Columns were knitting needles sunk into 40 thou drilled out blocks.

The fencing round the cluster of out-buildings at the London end was 30 thou, scribed both sides to prevent warping. There were problems incurred with the many roofs at the London end and the photograph on this page shows those on the prototype.

Painting: doors, lamps, brackets, drain-pipes, posts, seats, columns, outer window frames, framing on wooden outbuildings— Southern Railway green; valancing, fences and planking on wooden outbuildings— cream. The plastered walls on the platform side were painted with cream gloss which had been liberally sprinkled with talcum powder to "matt" down but unfortunately

Wokingham: main buildings

still shone too much. All brickwork was dark red, including the chimneys; the panels round windows and doorframes and on the curved wings on the pointed walls were picked out with cream. Roofs and platform were L.M.S. medium grey as were parapets round ladies' and the forward-jutting building on the yard side.

There is a rumour that Wokingham is to be demolished and the B.R.-type prefabricated platform shelters erected in its place so I am glad I modelled the station before it was too late.

Rotherfield and Mark Cross was opened in 1880, being the first station on the "Cuckoo Line" which diverged from the Tunbridge Wells West-Lewes line south of Eridge at Redgate Mill Junction. Its architecture was similar to all the stations on the now closed Cuckoo line except that at Hailsham which was also the longest open, only closing in 1968, the remainder of the line having been closed to passenger traffic in 1965. There are, in fact, another thirteen of the Rotherfield type of station after counting those on the Cuckoo line. I wish now that I had modelled Midhurst as it was, to me, the most interesting of the bunch, but the only drawing I could obtain then was of Rotherfield in the March 1960

Model Railways News and so Rotherfield it had to be.

The first parts to be modelled so as to get into the swing of a rather intricate building were the Gents' court, coal store and entrance to stationmaster's house, these being to the left of the main block when viewed from the platform side. The location of the ancillary buildings differed from station to station in this type of architecture. This wing was made from three layers of 40 thou, scribed inside and out; the doors were scribed for panelling on the middle layer and in the case of the house entrance the rather oriental-shaped transom was removed and a 10 thou frame backed by 10 thou glazing stuck in place. Copings were 40 thou, scribed every 3 mm; roofs were 30 thou with 10 thou strips at 9 mm intervals.

The shell of the main block, the stationmaster's house, was two layers of 40 thou. It was scribed for bricks up to the line of the vertical hanging tiles. The stonework round the windows was marked out before the brickwork was tackled and the outline of the stonework scribed; it was left white when the remainder of the building was painted. The heavy external frames on the upper windows were cut out from 40 thou and stuck in position and the inner frames made from two layers of 20 thou were painted (top, umber; lower, cream), stuck into place and 10 thou glazing added. Then began the longest job, that of attaching the hanging tiles. The rectangular type were marked out on a 10 thou sheet, scribed every 3 mm, cut into strips and then glued in position, starting at the lower layer; each succeeding layer was indented $1\frac{1}{2}$ mm. The round tiles were also 10 thou extracted from an office punch and laid on individually. When the tiles had set, the small roofs over the oriel windows were added from 30 thou.

View under platform canopy

Rotherfield: Station Master's house

The long wing which originally boasted the refreshment room was built last. This was scribed for bricks up to the mouldings below the eaves; window frames were 20 thou and doors built up from three layers of the same, the circular apertures and round tops to the windows being drilled out and glazing added behind. The porch entrance was rather elaborate and the raised mouldings were cut from 20 thou as were the ornamental barge-boards.

A first floor of 40 thou was put in position and instead of the usual flat roof on the s.m.'s house, 40 thou inner roofs were cemented *behind* the gables to prevent them bending back. The actual roofs were at first 30 thou, scribed for slates, but thanks to a letter in the May, 1969 *Railway Modeller*, I learned they should have been tiles. So I cleaned the paint from the roofs, cut 3 mm strips of 10 thou, scribed every 3 mm, and starting at the base of the roofs,

laid them one by one, overlapping 1 mm, up to the ridgetiles. These had also been removed but when the new roofing was finished were reglued with Evostik, being cut from a plastic traycloth and impervious to Humbrol 77.

The platform canopy has individually built-up girders which locate onto cut-down Airfix columns. The actual canopy was 30 thou, curved with difficulty to follow the platform, and the strips 10 thou. Valancing was 20 thou, scribed vertically, the circular parts punched out with a leather punch and the holes burned with a pin. This was not altogether successful as paint clogged the holes and when an attempt was made to clean them, the valancing became somewhat chipped.

The finished buildings were as usual stuck down to a base which formed the platform and raised as described for Wokingham. This time the thickness of the base was 30 thou, still 10 thou too thin!

Painting. The brickwork and tiles were painted a dark red which I have been told is pretty nearly the correct colour. Gutters, doors, drainpipes, oriel window frames and

Entrance porch

Rotherfield and Mark Cross: platform elevation

columns were painted G.W.R. chocolate. Remaining window frames, the porch, valancing, tops of columns, bargeboards, girders, and moulding under eaves, G.W.R. cream. Roofs over Gents' court, coal stores, s.m.'s entrance, platform canopy and platform, G.W.R. wagon grey. The main roofs were painted a lighter grey when tiling was effected, damp soot being smeared with fingertips over these expanses to simulate weathering.

The final touch was to spread Croid clear liquid glue over the end walls of the coal store and throw on various coloured flockpowders to represent creeper, then to add some floral effects to the s.m.'s garden. A year later I find that this glue does not wear well and the "flowers" are peeling off—I think Evostik will prove more successful in future.

Slinfold was on the Guildford-Horsham branch of the L.B.S.C.R., the last stop before Christs Hospital. It was opened on October 2, 1865, and closed on June 14, 1965. An excellent article by David Sillince on this line appeared in the *Railway Magazine* for March and April 1966. I find the stations on this branch very attractive and have plans to model either Bramley and Wonersh or Cranleigh, and Baynards, the

first two stations being very similar architecturally and to be found on the same L.B.S.C.R. drawing.

I worked to a drawing for stations at Rudgwick and Slinfold; but when consulting the two photographs I had obtained from Lens of Sutton, I discovered there was one great difference between the two stations—the design was completely reversed for Slinfold. Though it would no doubt have been simpler to model Rudgwick, especially when I was preparing my own 4 mm drawings, it was Slinfold I had decided on and so Slinfold it would be. Further differences came to light as work proceeded: the building housing the scullery, W.C.s, coal stores, etc., had, according to the photographic evidence, been altered from that shown on the contract drawing. I do not know whether this alteration was made at the time of building or later. I modelled it as shown on the drawing and so ended up with a hybrid station. All photographs I have seen of Rudgwick show a small platform canopy at Rudgwick whereas there does not seem to have been a canopy at Slinfold.

The wing containing the general waiting room was made first. The walls were two layers of 40 thou, ends fitting between

12

sides; there was of course no scribing as the walls are plastered. A larger amount of glue was used in the joins to make sure they were invisible. Slinfold had round-topped windows as opposed to the pointed variety at Rudgwick, as shown on the main drawing, and I duly rounded them. The inner walls have rectangular openings, 1 mm wider all round; the doors were scribed on the inner wall.

When the main wing had been built in the same way, complete with round-topped windows, floors were fitted and the two shells joined together. The five-sided booking office was constructed round a shaped floor and attached to the main building. I then made all the windows from 2 layers of 10 thou glazed with a similar thickness. The outer layer was $\frac{1}{2}$ mm narrower all round than the aperture and the inner layer $\frac{1}{2}$ mm narrower still. Humbrol no. 3 green was applied to the outer frames, the inner left white. When the paint was dry, the two layers were stuck together and to the glazing and finally behind the top layer of the walls. Painted tissue paper curtains were stuck behind the house windows, but unfortunately I sploshed glue all over one of the bedroom windows; this was corrected by smearing white poster paint inside the glazing to imply that the room was being redecorated. Each window-sill was angled back 1 mm and a strip 1 mm square added below. The bay consisted of three sides stuck round formers at ground level and just below the windows to simulate the seats with cupboards underneath often found in bays. The front door was painted and the jutting porch made from 40 thou and stuck in position.

A base was cut from 40 thou to serve as forecourt and platform. I scribed slabs 16 mm × 8 mm along the platform edge, cutting off the ramp and storing it until needed. The smaller outbuildings were added, the walls of all except the scullery being scribed for brickwork. I left the front yard wall bare as though I had no photograph of this elevation, I imagined it would be plastered to tone in with the remainder of the frontage. The 6 mm high plinth of 40 thou was added next round the entire set of buildings, the top angled back 1 mm.

Roofs were made from 30 thou scribed for slates, card templates being employed to make sure the dimensions on the tricky

Slinfold: rail elevation

parts were accurate before cutting from 30 thou. Mouldings under the eaves on the bay and booking office were built up from 30 thou strips. Ridging was 20 thou, guttering 10 thou. The ornamental barge-boards were set out in pairs; curves were formed round coins: note the semi-circular cut-outs on the front boards. Drainpipes were knitting needles and Airfix; the booking office vent was a knitting needle suitably bent.

The chimneys were not as difficult as at first appeared. I built the bases first, from 30 thou, none needing to be scribed. Moulding round the top was 10 thou × 2 mm; flashing was also 10 thou. The chimneys were of square section; all except those on the main building were scribed for bricks. Mouldings at the top of the stacks were 10 thou: 5 mm, 4 mm, 3 mm, and 1 mm wide stuck on in that order. Stacks were set at an angle to their bases—

Slinfold: booking hall

Slinfold road elevation

two side by side on the ladies' waiting room; four on the other wing. Pots were biro tubing. Finally steps were added at each door and parapets on the yard walls.

Painting: The main buildings were coated with poster paint mixed to the yellow-cream now used by the Southern Region. Care was taken to keep the walls grease-free and the paint was brushed on thickly. Where it "retreated" it was touched up when dry. Doors, guttering, vent, drainpipes and "pole" over porch were painted Humbrol no. 3 green. Bargeboards were cream.

The model was raised to platform height and treated to a parana pine base as described for Wokingham. After this I spent a couple of days detailing the platforms. The original L.B.S.C.R. nameboard had been utilised at Slinfold and the usual enamel plate screwed over. I built this nameboard, scribed on the original planks and added a newly-painted enamel plate of 10 thou. The name was affixed by Letraset. Posts were 3 mm square, the capping built up from various thicknesses. Fencing and access gate were Airfix and Playcraft. I left the lantern off the gas-lamp, though I had noted the lamp further up the platform was still complete. The hanging lamp was an Airfix lamp top, with wire

burned in, bent round, and then cemented with Evostik through a no. 68 hole drilled in the upper storey. The Way Out sign over the general waiting room door was stuck to a pin and again through a 68 hole. The lone telegraph pole, with the correct number of crossbars, was sunk through the platform. Timetables and blank advertisement boards were made from 20 thou, painted green and black. Two platform barrows, a green Merit station seat, and a bucket completed the picture.

Chichester station is on the Brighton–Portsmouth west coast line of the L.B.S.C.R. It was opened on June 8th 1846, was scheduled to be rebuilt in the 1938 electrification scheme but, Hitler's machinations having prevented this, it was reconstructed by B.R. in the late 1950s; I am not certain of the exact rebuilding date but the idea was mooted in 1957 judging by a letter in the *Railway Magazine* for April of that year when the correspondent hoped that the cupola over the ticket collectors' room could be incorporated into the proposed new building. This letter is the first friendly reference to the old station I have encountered: when I told various fellow members of the H.M.R.S. that I intended modelling the original station I was greeted with such remarks as: "Why build that dirty old place ?'' and "The worst collection of buildings I've ever come across—and that subway . . . !''

Well, maybe they were right, but from a modelling point of view I have yet to discover a more diverse and interesting set of buildings. I have included Chichester among the brickbuilt stations, but in truth it had brick, wooden and corrugated iron edifices, with as many contrasting roofs.

I had great difficulty in obtaining photographs of Chichester in its original form. R. C. Riley kindly loaned me a photograph taken by C. R. L. Coles *c.* 1947 looking towards Portsmouth; an earlier view facing the same direction was published in *Railway World* in July 1956 to accompany part one of an article entitled *The L.B.S.C.R. West Coast Line* by H. C. P. Smail. This article continued in the August and September magazines and was expanded from a two-part article in the *Sussex County Magazine* in 1954. The only other photograph I could locate was on page 5 of *The Hundred of Manhood and Selsey Tramways* by Edward Griffith.

The accompanying drawings were scaled up from a copy of an official L.B.S.C.R. plan dated December 1914. This plan showed only side elevations and so a ground plan of the same survey was purchased also. Of course this did not give heights of end elevations, and windows in these sections have had to be worked out from typical Chichester dimensions.

Having gained a fairly intimate knowledge of the various buildings on the down side (or Portsmouth side) from this drawing session, I laid a sheet of 40 thou, formed of two 26″ × 16″ pieces cemented together "end on", on the dining table preparatory to marking out the ground plan of each building ready for "keying" them into place as they were completed. There is a gradual descent of 4 mm from the London to the Portsmouth end of the down side. I was therefore faced with the prospect of either graduating the base or raising each building the required amount of millimetres, taking the top of the retaining wall as an inverted datum line. After much thought, I marked out the buildings on the base as originally planned; the extra millimetres would be added to the structures and the ground filled in round each.

The ground plan started just east of the water tower and finished at the ramp situated halfway along the platform signal cabin; the plan also incorporated the platform and due allowance was made for the width of this and of the retaining wall which stretched from the water tower to partway along the ticket collectors' room. This wall did not run straight, there being a "kink" between the footwarmers' heater room and the porters' room. I have included a ground plan of this wall section to make it clear. When the wall and buildings had been drawn, the platform was cut away and put in store.

The first parts of the station to be built were the heater room and the short section of retaining wall from water tower to left wall of porters' room. This wall formed the fourth wall of all buildings on the down side except that of ticket collectors' room. It was made from three layers of 40 thou, the two outer layers scribed for bricks; door and window apertures were removed, the frames and arches being left plain. Note that (a) the framing and panelling on either side of door was different; (b) the bullnose blue bricks on top of retaining wall; these came 1½ mm down from top of wall and were scribed every 1 mm along, the scribing mark being carried over when the layers are stuck together and dry. This top was sanded to a round section to simulate shape of bricks. Entrance door was formed by the centre of the three layers and 10 thou panelling cemented in place. The heater room was made from 40 thou, two layers for the side and gable end, one thickness only where end butts onto porters' room. Scribed where brickwork shows, the gable end was pigeonholed; I drilled these holes but when the building was finished, pondered whether thin slits would have been more correct: I always get these notions too late! The three sides were assembled round a floor and to the retaining wall. Window frame of 10 thou stuck to scribed 10 thou glazing was fitted into aperture on platform side, and when dry a flat roof was added. Actual roof was 30 thou, scribed for slates; overhang only on yard side which was also shaped to receive chimney. This was made from 40 thou, scribed for bricks, with 20 thou × 1 mm strip round top; pot—biro tubing. Ridging: 10 thou × 1½ mm; bargeboards: 20 thou × 2 mm.

The longest individual task came next— the remainder of the retaining wall. This was joined at nearly three quarters its length and I made the joint in a different place on each layer for added strength. All door and window apertures were removed; doors without windows were left blank on the two lower layers, otherwise aperture was cut out on each layer, doors being built up of 20 thou later. Note cut-outs on panelling on platform side of stables; at that point the retaining wall was 4 mm thick and the panels recessed 2 mm. Bullnose bricks scribed out as for short section. On yard side brickwork was only scribed where it will show between and above buildings. On the platform side, the entire wall was scribed from 9 mm up from base. When all scribing, removal of doors and windows had been completed on both outer layers, it was stuck under pressure for over a day. It was then stuck to the prepared base, making sure it stood at right angles to this and left for a further day.

It will be seen that doors and windows on the platform side vary considerably, some with glass, some plain. When 10 thou panelling was not indicated, the doors were scribed with a no. 3 blade and then cleaned. Some transoms required frames, others were plain glass. Door to subway was made from a central 20 thou piece with the bars carefully cut out and sandwiched between 10 thou layers. This door was modelled partially open for a more realistic effect. Window frames were painted when stuck to glazing, were scribed when dry and inserted into apertures. A deep cream colour was used on window frames which would contrast with the paler brickwork. All stonework round doors and windows was left white and acquired a weathered look under constant handling. The final portion of the retaining wall was of wooden construction and this was added last, scribed for planking, the overlays being 20 thou.

The porters' room came next. Side fitted between ends. Side was two layers of 40 thou; west end two layers of 40 thou, east end one layer. Brickwork was scribed on, which did not take long as the building butts onto stables, heater room and fowl house; it also adjoins greenhouse but as bricks would be visible through the glass, they were scribed on. It was assembled round 40 thou floor and to retaining wall and a flat roof fitted. Roof was built as for heater room. Chimney 40 thou, scribed for bricks, with 20 thou × 1 mm strip round top; biro tubing was used for pot and 20 thou discs arranged on top for cowling. Bargeboards were 20 thou × 2 mm.

Water-softening tank was built from three layers of 40 thou, both outer layers scribed for bricks. Four sides were assembled onto ground plan and well stuck down; joints were scribed round when set. Fowl house located on top of tank wall nearest platform. It was built of 40 thou, scribed vertically for planking every 2 mm. The side door was scribed at 1 mm intervals and given a frame 20 thou × 1 mm. Black 30 thou was used for roof to represent tarred roofing felt.

Stables. Four layers of 40 thou were employed on the yard wall: two for panel overlays, one for main wall which has window apertures, the fourth to prevent warping of third. Second layer was scribed only up to 6 mm to form plinth, first and third where necessary, noting where fodder store came; scribing began 6 mm up to allow for plinth. Door was scribed vertically for planking on fourth layer and a 10 thou × 1 mm frame glued in place. Rounded tops of windows and door were scribed with old pair of dividers, broken out and cleaned. Window frames were 10 thou, stuck to 10 thou glazing which was scribed for bars and then fixed in position behind third layer.

Ends were two layers, of 40 thou, scribed where brickwork showed; they fitted between retaining and yard walls. No floor was necessary as building was very strong, but a flat roof was fitted. Roof was 30 thou, scribed for slates; vent on crown of roof built up from 40 thou, heavily scribed to represent slits; strip 30 thou × 1 mm cemented all round halfway up vent; roof 20 thou. Ridging on stable roof 10 thou × 2 mm, bargeboards 20 thou × 3 mm.

Refreshment Room Coals: This was integral with outside wall of Manure Pit; gabled end forms east wall of pit. Pit walls were 3 mm thick, scribed on both sides, with bullnose bricks on top as on retaining wall. Coals walls were two layers of 40 thou, scribed for bricks; door planking scribed on lower layer and 10 thou × 1 mm frame added. No rear wall was required as Coals butts onto refreshment room. Roof 30 thou, scribed for slates with a 1 mm overlap at each end. 40 thou step fitted.

Chichester: view across from down to up side

Refreshment Room: This building was raised 2 mm to allow for rise in ground, therefore brick base is 7 mm high. Walls made from 2 layers of 40 thou, top layer scribed for planking from 7 mm up. Rear window has 10 thou frame 2 mm wide round aperture on outside as well as normal 10 thou inside window frames; 10 thou glazing, the bars scribed on; sill 1 mm square, overlapping framing by 1 mm each side. Sides were assembled round floor and to retaining wall. Framing round building was 10 thou, 3 mm wide. Flat, false roof was fitted and strips, 40 thou × 15 mm, stuck on top to overhang roof by 5 mm on three sides and thus forming eaves. Modillons were made as described for Eastbourne. Roof was 30 thou, scribed for slates and stuck to top of eaves. The chimney section up to the eaves was made from four layers of 40 thou, each marked out the same, but only the top one scribed for bricks. When dry, chimney was cemented in place on wall and brickwork continued along side to wall. Upper half was seated on roof, making sure it lined up with lower part. It was also built of 40 thou, scribed for bricks where appropriate. Top was formed from 20 thou strips, filled with Plasticine to receive the cowl (biro-tubing); the coxcomb was a dab of Evostik. Lantern roof was made from four pieces of 40 thou; ends were scribed vertically, sides horizontally and deeply to represent vents; overlays were 10 thou as were the ridging and flashing. Flat roof was fitted to lantern with a 2 mm overhang all round; actual roof 30 thou, scribed for slates. Finally a 7 mm plinth was made from 40 thou, scribed for bricks and stuck in position with plenty of glue. This wooden building was painted as follows: planking—deep poster cream, the same colour as all window frames on the station; vertical and horizontal framing, outside window frame and eaves—umber; chimneys and plinths—cream emulsion paint.

Subway: The strengthening pillars 2 mm thick were scribed for bricks and cemented in position on retaining wall. Subway walls were 3 mm thick, scribed for sides, bullnose bricks on top. Subway door was painted before roof glazing was added. Steps formed from pieces of 40 thou ranging from 57 mm–33 mm long at 4 mm intervals, painted stone colour. Urinals (for use on race days only) door is in rear wall of subway which is common to both. Glazing over subway is 10 thou stuck under a frame of 20 thou and attached to walls and retaining wall. Urinals walls also 3 mm thick, scribed on every side except that next to refreshment room to which it is glued. Again bullnose bricks are on top. Floor of 60 thou fitted 7 mm up on 40 thou formers to bring it nearer platform level. 10 stalls made from 20 thou, 24 mm × 5mm.

The entrance door located between the end subway wall and the waiting room block was painted next as it would be impossible to reach it when the final block of buildings was built.

Toilets, Waiting Rooms, Collectors, etc.: As with the refreshment room, two layers of 40 thou were used for this wooden building. The entire length of what in plan appears to be two buildings was cut out in one piece for strength. The toilet block had retaining wall as fourth side, whereas part of collectors' block extended beyond end of retaining wall. The yard wall was scribed for planking when door and window apertures had been removed; note different height and size of collectors' windows. These buildings were again raised 3 mm to allow for rise in ground, the extra 3 mm being added to plinth height. Five interior partitions were put in for strength, plus double end wall of collectors'. Platform side of collectors' was made next; little scribing was necessary due to dwarf wall, timetables and nameboard. Roof of waiting room block made as that of refreshment room, as were eaves and modillons; framing and plinths were treated in similar fashion. When the waiting room building had been completed, I realised there should have been two windows at the Portsmouth end: it was then too late. Gable end of collectors' from 40 thou, top layer scribing for vertical planking; this was stuck to the flat, false roof of 40 thou, with a 3 mm overhang on 3 sides. When dry, the actual roof was cemented in position. This roof was made from 30 thou covered with 10 thou, the boarding strips being 10 thou × 1 mm. The platform side has two skylights; apertures were cut and frames of 10 thou inserted, stuck to 10 thou glazing. 10 thou frames were also formed round skylights. Chimneys were built up from scribed 40 thou, with 20 thou × 1 mm strips round top, and biro-tubing pots. The cupola base was made from 20 thou;

Chichester: rear of stables and water towers   Platform elevation—down side

Down side ladies' and waiting rooms

floor and flat roof were 40 thou with cutouts at the corners to receive 1 mm square struts. Dome was taken from Tri-ang M7 which had been converted to D3; the bell came from an Airfix station lamp. The valance which ran round three sides of the collectors' was made from 30 thou, the sawtooth edge being nicked with a shortened no. 1 blade. It fitted under the overhanging eaves.

The final construction on the toilet block was the awning over the entrance. This was formed from a 40 thou rectangle, surrounded by 30 thou valancing carefully cut out with shortened no. 1 blade; the

mouldings round the top of the valances were 10 thou strips of 2 mm and 1 mm wide respectively.

To complete the down side buildings on the base, the conservatory, oil and fodder stores were made next. The lower part of the conservatory was two layers of 40 thou, scribed for bricks where they would show. The glazed part was built from 20 thou stuck to 10 thou glazing, the narrow bars being scribed on. The door was also 20 thou, painted umber. Brickwork was painted cream but the upper part left white as I had no idea what colour the L.B.S.C.R. painted greenhouses!

Oil and fodder stores had a 40 thou shell, the doors being scribed on. Corrugations were made from "Battle" cocktail sticks. These were rather overscale but convincing. I had no fortune in obtaining the celebrated corrugated tinfoil: Ken even telephoned the manufacturers in London, but was told the material was no longer available. Oil store roof was 20 thou; fodder store black 30 thou.

This completed the down side buildings except for the signal cabin and water tower. To raise the base to its required height an extra layer of 40 thou was stuck in position from London wall of water softening tank to end of platform; a further layer from London wall of refreshment room coal store, and a final layer from London wall of urinals. The obvious "step" was sanded until it became a slight slope. The stableyard was filled with glue and cobbles scribed on. Ramps were added at the platform access doors and sanded until an invisible join ensued. All "ground" was painted dark grey, except of course the rolling way outside refreshment room; this was made of 10 thou, with 10 thou frame and painted brown. The short wall behind signal cabin from London end of collectors' was three layers of 40 thou, scribed for bricks and the bullnose capping; plinths were 40 thou, angled back at top.

Oil and fodder stores, collectors' roof and fowl house now were painted thick loco black; chimney pots were also liberally splashed with this paint. All brickbuilt structures were coated with cream emulsion paint, while the bullnose bricks were painted G.E.R. blue. Anthracite soot was liberally applied to all walls and roofs and worked in by finger.

The platform was fitted next, the edging having been scribed every $1\frac{1}{2}$ mm to a width of 3 mm. Chichester had notoriously low platforms and at some period of their history were raised to a more correct level; I have been unable to ascertain the date of this rise, so have modelled them low. Strips of 40 thou 9 mm wide were cemented at base of retaining wall and under platform and the latter glued into position. The ramp at the London end was fixed in place on 40 thou formers and the join made as inconspicuous as possible. Brickwork on platform face left for an all-out effort when remainder of station was completed. The rectangular hole where the signal cabin

would locate was surrounded by layers of 40 thou to bring the area up to the correct height: as will be seen from plans and photographs, the signal cabin is situated by the platform and access ramps.

Signal cabin: I include this here rather than in the chapter devoted to these structures as it is an integral part of the station. The shell was two layers of 40 thou; inner layer comes to within 1 mm of windows on three sides and right up to roof at rear. Sides were scribed for bricks and planking where appropriate. Door in base at Portsmouth end was scribed on lower layer and a 10 thou × 1 mm framing added. Four sides were assembled round floor and when dry, a 40 thou plinth, scribed for bricks and angled back 1 mm at top, was stuck on. Door to upper floor was scribed on top layer, also with 10 thou framing. Framing round planking on this floor 10 thou × 2 mm. Window frames were cut from 20 thou and stuck to 10 thou glazing scribed for thinner bars. Note outer windows at front slide *behind* inner ones. Floor of cabin was stuck in place; a lever frame made from two layers of 60 thou and sanded to shape was put in next, complete with levers made from burned-in household pins, and Airfix signalman. Desk built from scraps of styrene, stove from Brittains' poplar tree trunk. Flat roof was cemented in, followed by another of 30 thou with an overhang of 3 mm all round. Roof was 30 thou, scribed for slates; ridging being 10 thou strips. Stovepipe was biro tubing with "nib" glued through hole drilled in roof. Vent was made from fanshaped piece in biro, the conical part being shaped up from Plasticine. Steps came from an Airfix windmill sail locating onto 40 thou platform. Banisters were 20 thou cut in one piece. The brickwork was painted red, as shown in a colour slide loaned me by Peter Barker of Copenhagen. Indeed, without these slides of the platform signal cabin I doubt whether it could have been built as I had no side elevations at all. Incidentally, a mirror is shown on the C. R. L. Coles photograph already mentioned. This has not been modelled as I do not know whether it was there in 1910; obviously it was used to see along the track past the footbridge. Planking on the cabin was cream poster paint; framing, steps and banisters, umber; roof, grey.

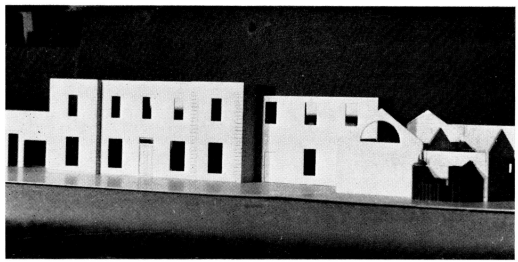

Chichester: up side under construction

Refreshment room and Parcels

The dwarf wall in front of the collectors' was built now, having had to wait until the platform was in situ. It was 3 mm wide, scribed at the front for ordinary and bullnose bricks. Nameboard and timetables were made from 30 thou with 10 thou × 1 mm strips for divisions and framing; all were given a coat of black paint. Lettering on nameboard came from various Letrasets; timetables were left blank until later.

All having been completed on the base, I turned to the water tower which would eventually locate into cut-outs in the short retaining wall section. Four layers of 40 thou were required for each wall, ends to fit between sides. Top two layers are virtually the same, except that second layer formed plinth; this was the only part that needed scribing, but whole of top layer was scribed. Third layers were scribed in panels and window apertures removed. Fourth layer was plain except for larger apertures. Door at London end was made from two layers of 20 thou and located behind fourth layer. All glazing was 10 thou, the bars being scribed on and the windows stuck behind the third layer. 40 thou floor and flat roof were fitted, plus two extra layers at top to receive tank. Keystones above windows were strips of 40 thou, sanded to shape, sills were 1 mm square. Tank was made from plain 40 thou assembled round a 40 thou floor and, when dry, the characteristic curve was sanded at the base. 10 thou × $\frac{1}{2}$ mm vertical strips were added and then whole structure was stuck in place. Brickwork was painted cream emulsion, dirted when dry. Door, umber; tank, dark grey inside and outside. The water softening plant was a 40 thou box which had cut-outs on top and bottom to fit into yard side of water tower. It was poster painted a light concrete colour and again dirtied when dry.

Remainder of platform was built as already described for buildings section except that it was curved—a straight platform would have been easier to model but it would not then have looked like Chichester. When the platform was finished and attached to the water tower, the entire down side section was glued onto a prepared baseboard with Evostik. Now it was possible to add the fence which abutted the water tower and formed a barrier to the bay platform. It was made from 30 thou, with 6″ planks scribed on both sides; overlays of 20 thou × 2 mm and 1 mm proud were fixed at each end to represent posts. It was painted cream and umber.

A ground plan was also drawn out on 40 thou for the up side; but as yard and platform were at same height the latter was left in place while the buildings were assembled. There was a retaining wall on the up side, its length being broken up by the main block of buildings. The platform elevation from parcels at the Portsmouth end to the telegraph office at the London end was made from one piece of 40 thou; the parts of this section which formed the retaining wall were then treated as on the down platform, remembering to build up the cloakroom gable above the bullnose brick capping. Brickwork was scribed on this long section and door and window apertures removed as on down side. 40 thou inner layers of buildings were cut shorter to allow for right angled walls to key in behind first layer. Second layer of retaining

wall also added at this stage and while these dried, the final layer was scribed and then stuck on under pressure. At the London end, the last section was set back 2 mm, so the bottom layer of main section became *top* layer of extra part and so was scribed on front. Last section at Portsmouth end was also set back 2 mm, but this section was built as retaining wall on down side and stuck in position when parcels side wall was in position. The square end pillar was made from 40 thou, scribed for bricks; the pointed top was four pieces of 20 thou set on a 30 thou base.

The first building on the up side to be tackled was the booking hall and station-master's house. As the platform wall was already prepared, the four side walls were next made, all locating into platform wall for strength; they were two layers of 40 thou, scribed for bricks where necessary, the corners left bare to receive quoins later. The window at the London end was calculated from photographs. The two short and one long front walls were constructed and when all were thoroughly dry, assembly began. Three floors of 40 thou were cut and glued to base and rear wall; the two side walls of each flanking wing were cemented to their floor, rear and front walls. Finally, the long front wall was stuck to its floor and to the inner side walls of the wings. Lower window frames were two thicknesses, 20 lower, 10 upper; main horizontal bar was 10 thou; remaining bars were scribed on 10 thou glazing. Doors were panelled as appropriate. When windows were securely in place, white serviettes were cut up for net curtains on bottom part of first floor windows and affixed with Evostik; blue serviette curtains were then stuck on either side of upper windows. Inner dividing walls were then added, followed by ceilings and flat roof. The decorative mouldings round the windows on the yard elevation were various thicknesses of styrene strip. The quoins were 20 thou × 4 mm, alternately 9 mm and 6 mm long; each quoin was bevelled by sanding before being stuck in place, thereby improving the effect. Modillons were 20 thou × 2 mm, top piece 3 mm and bottom piece 6 mm long; 30 thou × 1 mm strip was fixed below these. Strips of 40 thou overhanging 8 mm all round were glued to flat roof to take roofs at a later stage.

View from up to down side

Attention was turned to the refreshment room; the two outside walls were usual layers of 40 thou, scribed where necessary; the third wall which butted onto booking hall section was left plain and added only for squareness. Walls were assembled round 40 thou floor; windows, doors, etc., were constructed to same stage as main block.

Cloaks and parcels room walls were measured, scribed and prepared; the wall nearest to refreshment room overlaps the yard wall by 5 mm. The large semi-circular window was scribed with an old pair of dividers, snapped out and cleaned carefully; 10 thou glazing, scribed for vertical bars, was stuck behind window frame; it was held until dry to prevent bowing.

The last brick building at the Portsmouth side was the Gents' and was built from 40 thou as usual; windows were calculated from Gents' at Littlehampton. Only two walls were necessary as retaining wall forms third and cloaks fourth walls. Floor was cut from 40 thou.

Refreshment room stores and extra parcels room believed to be one building as far as outside dimensions go. It was constructed in the same way as the wooden buildings on the down side, the planking being carried up to the ridge. All four walls were modelled and both ends have gables. Again window and door heights were calculated from other doors and windows on the up side. It was painted as down side wooden buildings.

Stores hut was built like the fodder store on down side except for the windows: these were cut from 10 thou, carefully forming the rounded tops.

The Ladies' and telegraph office at the London end were brick-built and modelled in the usual manner.

Roofs: The first to be made was that on the refreshment room stores which had a plain roofing felt finish; it was 30 thou, the skylight made as on the collectors' and painted thick black. The parcels roof was also 30 thou, this time scribed for slates, carefully cut out to fit onto r.r. stores roof. Gents' likewise 30 thou scribed for slates, fitted into overhang on parcels. Ladies' and telegraph office roofs 30 thou, scribed for slates. Dormer on Ladies' built up from 20 thou, with 10 thou overlay and 10 thou glazing. 30 thou extra layer on dormer roof, sanded to curve. Refreshment room roof made of three pieces of 30 thou, scribed for slates; it located just under eaves on main block. The roofs on this block were made last. First the long sections back and front were cut from 30 thou, scribed for slates; the front piece, though not wholly visible, was modelled the same length as the rear one for strength. Next came the outside pieces: the length of

23

the ridge on these pieces is equal to the length of the jut on the wings. When these were dry, the inner side pieces were cut to shape and finally the front triangular sections were glued in place.

Chimneys: All were built up from 40 thou, scribed for bricks, narrow ends between sides. The decorative mouldings round the tops were built up to suit. The large chimney on the London end of the main block is built in two sections: the first up to the eaves, the second, carefully lined up, on the roof itself. Ten thou was used for all flashing, for the thick lead strips at the base of the main block roof, and for ridging.

Extensions to platforms built as for down side; the ramp at the London end had four pieces cut out to receive footbridge supports. All platform facing made from 20 thou scribed for bricks.

Bookstall: The counter was made from 20 thou on 40 thou frame, curved at corners. Rear walls were 40 thou. It was decked out with oblongs from newspaper stippled with various watercolours. Airfix assistant presided.

Posters and timetables: As station was modelled in 1910 period, the *Railway Magazine* for this year was borrowed from the H.M.R.S. library and seven contemporary advertisements for different railways scaled down onto paper and painted. They were then stuck on card, given an umber border and fixed in appropriate positions on both sides of the station with Evostik. Timetables from the Merco sheet were cut and adapted; the newsbills from this sheet were stuck to the front of the bookstall. Remainder of advertisements came from M.R.A.S. sheet, stuck onto 20 thou, given an umber border, and glued to walls with 77.

Canopies: These were 50 mm wide; part which depended from retaining wall was glazed. The frame for the glazed sections was a sandwich; top: 10 thou; glazing 20 thou,; bottom 30 thou. London ends were 48 mm wide × 50 mm × 24 mm × 10 mm × 40 thou. scribed at 3 mm intervals. The v-sections were cut out with shortened no. 1 blade, the holes being no. 68. Valancing was 30 thou × 10 mm deep, no. 68 hole 3 mm up at 3 mm intervals; v-sections made as at ends. Canopy support beams were 3 mm × 1 mm. Columns came from cocktail sticks set in no. 46 holes drilled at 80 mm intervals in platform.

Bases were biro tubing slipped down columns and Evostik-ed in place. Zinc boarding sections of canopies were 40 thou, curved to conform with platform radius; 10 thou × 1 mm strips were laid on at 12 mm intervals and along top and bottom. Columns and canopy supports painted umber; ends and valancing, cream poster; canopy top, dark grey.

Footbridge: This was made from an Airfix kit, plus two extra of the long stairs and girder sections adapted to fit location. All girder cross-pieces were sawn out and bridge assembled with two straight flights on the up side and one oblique flight on down. Legs of bridge locate into pre-cut holes in ramp on up platform. Plastic mesh from a bag which had contained nuts was used as filling between struts; this material took plastic glue. The bridge was painted umber, except for steps which were dark grey, and the underneath and smoke deflectors which were black.

Level crossing: The gates were Airfix, three sections to each. End-posts were extended upwards and a corner bracket added of 20 thou, with hole drilled through. Gateposts were 36 mm × 3 mm × 3 mm set into Airfix bases. The gates were stuck together at centre and a 10 thou disc, painted red with a white outer ring, was cemented on the railway side. Brackets were painted black, as were the support wires from gateposts to below disc. Gates and posts were painted white.

All platform faces were painted dark brown-red. Fencing from London end of retaining wall to footbridge was made of 30 thou, scribed each side every 2 mm. 20 thou posts were added at 36 mm intervals, 2 mm wide. It was painted cream and umber. Similar fence built on down side from near footbridge to edge of baseboard. Polyfilla was mixed and applied on down side to merge styrene "ground" with baseboard at correct level. A strip of paving was fixed outside fencing and all this part was painted dark grey. Similarly, strips of wood and a Polyfilla mix were employed on the up side to bed the styrene base in properly and then painted dark grey. Streamline track was laid and set in Kings Cross ballast and rail-built buffer stops added as necessary. And so, after about two months' constructional work, Chichester was completed except for water columns.

Stone-built stations

Knitsley. This model was built for the H.M.R.S. stand at the Northern Railway Exhibition, Harrogate, in 1968. The station was on the Lanchester valley branch of the North Eastern Railway and had been closed to passengers in 1939 and to freight in 1966. Architecture on this line closely resembled that on the same railway's Harrogate–Pateley Bridge branch—which was why I chose the station. I worked to drawings and photographs by W. Fawcett in the October 1967, *H.M.R.S. Journal.* An article on the Nidd Valley Branch by David Jenkinson was published in *Model Railway News* for April 1957.

This was my first attempt at a stone-built station in styrene sheet and I must confess I wondered whether it would work. Scribing bricks is one thing, scribing stones quite another.

All courses except around window and door apertures and at each corner were marked out 2 mm deep. Those around apertures and corners were 4 mm deep. The vertical divisions were marked out more at random—the block lengths varying between 6 and 30 inches. As the sides were short, it was no great matter to pencil in all the blocks before scribing them. The horizontal courses were scribed first, each indentation being made, cleaned out, and then remade, giving a deeper and slightly wider cut than brickwork to emphasise the rougher finish; the vertical courses followed the same method. All sides were built 3 mm thick, windows locating behind the third layer. Yard and platform walls were made 3 mm short at each side as they fitted between the ends; with regard to these ends: care was taken to get the "step" effect correctly shaped, the rounded parts being sanded when all three layers were dry. The four walls were assembled round a 40 thou floor, plenty of glue being used to hide the joins. When this "box" was dry, the stonework was carried round the corners and the joins made invisible.

Window frames were made from two layers, the top of 20 thou, the lower of 10 thou which included the sash bar; vertical bars were scribed on the 10 thou glazing.

The entrance porch was constructed like the main building, except that the ends fit between front and main walls. Doors were made from two layers of 20 thou, located behind second wall layer, with 10 thou glazing for transoms.

The bay window on the platform side was built from two layers of 40 thou, the lower parts scribed for stonework. Care was needed to get the window frames in the unusual cavity; the middle one was offered up first, followed by two flanking frames—all frames themselves made as rest on this building. A stone sill of 40 thou was added, chamfered to fit into main walls. False roof was put in place to prevent warping and actual roof was cut from three pieces of 30 thou, scribed for slates. Two layers of eaves cut from 30 thou strips; flashing was 10 thou.

A 40 thou first floor was glued in place; before the flat roof was treated in like manner, tissue curtains were Evostik-ed over the lower halves of the upper windows. The main roof was 30 thou, scribed for slates. Chimneys were built up from 40 thou, scribed for stonework, the pots being cut from 10 thou.

The outer buildings were built as already described for the main part; the urinal, w.c. and lamp room have skylights; these were given 10 thou frames and glazed behind with 10 thou. There was no door to the urinals and a plain inner wall was added to divide this part from the w.c. The vents on these two offices were scribed on the second layer of the outer wall, as shown in photograph. Coal store door was scribed on the second layer, a 20 thou frame being added, 1 mm wide.

At this stage, the whole model was cemented down to a base of 80 thou. When it was thoroughly dry, a plinth of 40 thou was glued right round buildings, scribed for stonework. Cut-outs were left for the drainpipes which were knitting needles.

Painting: This again presented a problem as it was some years since I had seen the Nidd Valley stations. I mixed a pale stone colour from Humbrol paints and washed it over the entire stonework, brushing in a little thinners here and there to make the weathered effect so often found on stone structures. Roofs were dark grey; doors, outer window frames, vents and drainpipes—chocolate. When the paintwork had dried, I applied wet soot with a finger, working it into the stonework as I hoped soot would

Knitsley: yard elevation

Platform elevation

Close-up of bay

End elevation

have permeated: the finished result was quite convincing.

Saltaire was also built for the 1968 Harrogate exhibition. I had looked through back numbers of the modelling magazines for a suitable Yorkshire station and came across an article and drawing by Derek Naylor in the February 1966 *Model Railway News* devoted to this station on the Skipton–Leeds line of the Midland Railway. Alas, there is no longer a trace of Saltaire to be seen.

This was another stone building, but of quite a different character. First part made was the rear elevation as it was the simplest —the entire back wall was completely devoid of window or door! This was made in one piece, stonework being scribed out as for Knitsley, though without the larger stones round apertures and on corners. The front elevation was tackled next; the two walls flanking the central section were marked out and scribed for stonework, the door and window apertures being removed; the curved tops to the window apertures were scored with dividers, cracked out and then cleaned up. Window frames were cut from 10 thou, each pane being removed with a very sharp no. 1 blade. These frames were then stuck to 10 thou glazing. The door was two layers of 20 thou, the panelling being cut out from the top layer.

The next step was to make the gabled central wall; a large aperture to take the bay was removed and the short side walls cut and scribed. Before making the bay, the end walls of the main section were marked out and scribed and all walls made thus far assembled round a 40 thou floor, ends between sides. The bay was constructed from three pieces of 40 thou, two layers thick, and scribed for stonework. These three pieces were stuck together and to the main wall with plenty of glue and left to dry overnight. The joins were then cleaned up. Windows and frames were added, the flanking ones being plainer. A flat roof was added and the actual roof was three pieces of 30 thou, scribed for slates. Strips of 1 mm square fit at sill level across whole of platform elevation and also at base of each window and door arch. An 80 thou base was prepared and scribed for stone slabs; the completed section of the station was glued down; a 30 thou step was fitted to the main doorway.

The two wing buildings were next built in the same way as the rest. Platform seats in these two shelters were strips of 20 thou on 20 thou "legs". Flat roofs were fitted on all three sections and then the real roofs of 30 thou, scribed for slates. Skylights were made on each roof at the rear, framed in 10 thou, with 10 thou glazing. Eaves and bargeboards were 30 thou, plus 1 mm squares under the eaves for decoration; arch keystones were 20 thou. All flashing was cut from 10 thou.

Saltaire: "mind that chimney!"

Chimneys were built from 40 thou, scribed for bricks; biro tubing was used for pots. Doorway at left wing has no door, but door at opposite end of station was modelled from two layers of 20 thou, the panelling cut from the upper layer. Ventilators were built up from various thicknesses of styrene sheet, the four pieces which go to each top being carefully cut to size and well stuck together. The overlays at end of each roof were 30 thou × 3 mm. Drainpipes were made from cocktail sticks; gutters were 10 thou × 1½ mm.

Painting: doors, seats, gutters, drainpipes—maroon. Windows and roof overlays —cream. To ensure I mixed the correct colour for the stonework, I wrote to Mr. Naylor who kindly sent me a small piece of stone from the demolished station. When the paint had dried, the station was dirtied in the same way as Knitsley. Roofs and platform—dark grey. Advertisements were stuck to rear walls of shelters. I was thankful to learn later from Mr. Naylor, who saw the model at Harrogate, that I had managed to capture the right colour and atmosphere . . .

Wooden stations

Fittleworth station was situated on the Pulborough–Midhurst line of the L.B.S.C.R., being the first stop west. Like the other two stations on this short line, it was timber-built. Fittleworth was opened on September 2nd 1889 and closed February 7th 1955, though a goods service lasted until 1967 when the famous signal cabin at Hardham Junction, the last on stilts, was demolished and the connection removed. I had hoped to model Selham as well as Fittleworth and Petworth, but there are no extant plans of this station.

As stated above, this station was built entirely of wood except for the three chimneys and roof. It was a twin to Hampden Park (opened as Willingdon) and both stations had canopies similar to Oxted.

The drawing obtained did not show yard elevation and so window and door heights were calculated from those on platform elevation.

Platform wall was built first of 40 thou, scribed for planking, and continued to include wall of Gents'. Window and door apertures were removed. The wall was then stuck onto a further 40 thou piece, 1 mm shorter at each end and *not* including Gents' wall; window and door apertures on this piece were 1 mm larger all round to allow for location of windowframes behind first layer. Yard wall was made the same way. Both were left under pressure overnight to dry thoroughly. The two end walls were marked out and scribed for planking and for bricks where chimneys were set into the timber; central portion was left blank as a top layer of 40 thou, scribed for bricks, stands proud of the wall here.

When all four sides were dry, they were assembled, ends between sides, round a 40 thou floor. Outside window frames were 20 thou cut out in one piece and stuck to wall; 30 thou × 1 mm sills were fitted when frames were dry. Inside windowframes were also 20 thou, with 10 thou inner frame and glazing.

Vertical and horizontal framing was 20 thou × 2 mm; top section and eaves were built up from various thicknesses according to plan. Interior partitions and ceiling of 40 thou were fixed in position. Roof was 30 thou, scribed for slates, cut-outs for chimneys being removed. Chimneys were built up of 40 thou, scribed for bricks, the tops being moulded from buff Plasticine. Ridging and flashing were added from suitable widths of 10 thou.

Remainder of Gents' was constructed as main building, the wooden entrance being 40 thou, scribed both sides for planking, with 10 thou overlays.

The buildings were now stuck down to 40 thou base which later also formed the platform. The plinth was glued in position; lower layer 40 thou × 4mm, upper layer 40 thou × 2 mm.

The canopy was made as follows: 30 thou valancing was scribed for planking and then stuck round a piece of 40 thou and left to dry. Three formers were cut from 40 thou and sanded to shape of roof; these were glued to top of section already built. A rectangle of 20 thou cut to the right size was bound round a rolling pin with string and immersed first in boiling water and then put under the cold tap. After the string was removed, the styrene was dried and the resultant curve stuck to the formers and held down gently until the cement had set. 10 thou moulding strips were added round valance.

Fittleworth rail elevation

Motor train in platform

Square section columns were made from 40 thou, set in 20 thou bases. As the canopy stood proud of the actual building, it was attached by 40 thou strips at each end. Columns were glued to platform and when set, canopy was lowered onto them and cemented to 40 thou strips on walls and tops of columns.

Paint scheme: walls and valancing—cream; framing, eaves, outside window-frames and top layer of inside windowframes, sills, columns, doors, plinth and moulding strips—Southern Railway green; roof, platform and top of canopy—dark grey; chimneys—weathered red.

The platform was raised to correct height—see Wokingham.

Petworth was the next station west along the line and was the original terminus. It was opened on 10th October 1859, and closed on 7th February 1955. Not only was it the largest of the three wooden stations, but also the most highly decorated, notably in the diagonal planking above and below the main body of the building. From study of the L.B.S.C.R. drawing it appears that the platform canopy was intended to stretch the entire length of the station, but only the short section shown on my plan has appeared in any photograph I have seen. There was also an ornate affair of wrought-iron on the crown of the booking hall roof, but this was beyond my modelling powers to produce. Finally, the booking hall doors

c

appeared to have stained-glass, but I have left them plain on the model.

The platform wall was built first, care being taken to get the diagonal lines the correct way: it takes less time doing it correctly and slowly than by hurrying and having to disguise the wrong strokes—as I did! Otherwise the platform and side walls were made as for Fittleworth. Yard side walls were made in three pieces to allow for jutting booking hall; the two short side walls of the booking hall were made the same way.

When all walls were dry, a floor of 40 thou cut and the building assembled, ends fitting between sides. Doors were two layers of 20 thou, panelling cut out of top layer. Inside window frames were 10 thou stuck to 10 thou glazing, glazing bars being scribed on when dry. Outside framing round windows was two layers of 20 thou cut out intact, stuck together and then cemented to walls. Sills were 40 thou, 2 mm wide, fitted under lower part of frames. All vertical and horizontal framing on wall was 20 thou of suitable widths. See dimensioned drawing.

The structure built thus far was then stuck down onto a piece of 40 thou which would later form platform. Plinths were built up from layers of 40 thou. Eaves were also built up in layers, this time of 20 thou, the vertical mouldings being cut one by one, and stuck on with a pin and plenty of glue.

Interior partitions and ceiling of 40 thou fitted next. The roof was made from 30 thou, scribed for slates. The large platform side of the roof was made in one piece: there were eight pieces to the entire roof.

The chimneys were 40 thou, inner layer left plain; the tops were built up of 30 thou strips and shaped round pots (biro tubing) with Plasticine.

Lantern shell was 40 thou, scribed deeply and angled to represent slits. Framing was 20 thou. Flat roof of 40 thou was added for strength and actual roof was as usual 30 thou, scribed for slates. Ridging and flashing 10 thou of suitable widths.

Canopy: Valancing was 30 thou, scribed for planks; top of canopy was also 30 thou, made in two pieces and making a lopsided

Petworth—looking west

Petworth Yard elevation

V, the longer side being nearest station wall. Strips of 10 thou × 1 mm formed overlays. The columns were from Airfix station lamps, cut just below curved part. Brackets were 20 thou with hole drilled out; a washer of suitable diameter was slipped over each column before the brackets were fixed and then brought up and cemented to base of brackets with Evostik.

The station was painted gloss cream which was a mistake and the last time I used gloss paint on woodwork as it caused glare when photofloods were used. Framing, doors, window frames, plinths, eaves, columns, brackets, valance overlays—Southern Railway green. Roof, platform and canopy top—dark grey. Chimneys—dark red, liberally coated with anthracite soot.

See Wokingham for platform raising operation.

Bute Street station, Luton, was built for the H.M.R.S. stand at the 1969 Luton Model Railway Club Exhibition. I worked from drawings made by Bill Ibbott as part of the H.M.R.S. Bedfordshire Survey and photographs were loaned by John Gilbert. Bute Street was on the G.N.R. branch from Hatfield to Dunstable and though the line is still open for some goods traffic, the station has been razed and the site made into a car park.

Sides were built from 20 thou, all window apertures being cut with a new no. 1 blade.

Planking on lower panels and on upper and middle panels of ladies' were scribed on. An inner layer of 40 thou was stuck behind all the scribed parts to prevent warping. Vertical and top and bottom overlays were 40 thou, remainder 20 thou. Glazing was 5 thou which was a little thin but all that was obtainable at the time. This was stuck on before the 40 thou inner layer so that it could be dried under pressure as the combined thicknesses of top layer and glazing did not add up to 40 thou. Ends fitted between sides and were made the same way, the brickwork on the chimney being scribed on the actual end.

John Gilbert consulted a G.N.R. expert and had the paint for the station made up at his own business, Ogden & Cleaver, Luton. Top half of the buildings were painted dark stone.

The platform was made next of 40 thou measuring 544 mm × 116 mm. It was scribed for paving stones of 12 mm × 16 mm. Location of buildings was marked on and also that of columns.

When the four sides of each building had been assembled round a 40 thou floor, the resultant box was cemented to its place on the platform. As so much of these waiting rooms were glazed, I added some interior details. Partitions between ladies' waiting room and ladies' toilet were made of 40 thou, 1 mm lower than height of walls to take ceiling. Seats were stuck along each side wall made from 40 thou × 9 mm; a stove from a section of Brittains' poplar treetrunk, the "stovepipe" being cut half-through and bent backwards, was fitted in each waiting room, locating under chimneys. Interiors below the windows, including the seats, were painted dark brown. Then ceilings of 40 thou were cemented in position.

The lower parts of the exteriors and the thick framing were painted dark brown; to add a little period flavour, timetables and MRAS advertisements were stuck in place.

Brackets and columns were tackled next. These were built up of strips of 40 thou, mainly 3 mm wide; outside diagonal supports were straight, inner ones curved. The brackets were also built out from walls in same way. These columns are shown in the photograph. When completely set, the columns and brackets were stuck in place on the platform and, having carefully scraped away sufficient paint, on walls.

Attention was next turned to the valances. The two end sections were made first, as a trial run as these were of course considerably shorter than the side valances. Made from 30 thou, with the centre piece shaped to the roof angle, they were scribed for planking every 1½ mm and a no. 68 hole drilled in each plank; ideally these should have come on planks, but the drill slipped more easily into the declivity. The lower 3 mm below each scribe was

Bute Street: end elevation

cut right through with a shortened no. 1 blade.

The roof was made of 40 thou for strength, the skylight portions being removed and glazing with 5 thou. Slates were scribed over buildings, the remainder assumed to be roofing felt. The two roof halves were glued together and to the buildings and when set the end valances were stuck over. The canopy was 40 thou, with strip 40 thou × 4 mm located along centre

Waiting room—side elevation

underneath; this strip was cemented onto brackets and columns. The long side valances were made the same way as the ends—it took some time! They were stuck to the edge of the canopy and in front of end valance. Moulding strips of 10 thou were added at top and centre of valances.

Chimneys were 40 thou, top mouldings built up from 20 thou of various widths, pots being biro tubing. Vent over ladies' toilet was made from 20 thou sides, 40 thou ends, 5 thou glazing and 20 thou roof. Flashing was 10 thou × 1 mm.

Brackets, columns, underside of canopy and rear of valances painted dark brown; valances dark stone; platform, top of canopy and roof grey; chimneys and platform facing brown-red.

St. Albans. This waiting room was made from drawings by Malcolm Cross in the *Model Railway Constructor* for November 1962. It served platforms 2 and 3 but was demolished several years ago and a Modern Image structure built.

Model sides were two layers of 40 thou, the top one scribed for planks, the lower one 1 mm shorter at each end. Panelling beneath windows was scribed on lower layer and the window apertures made large enough on this layer to receive 10 thou frames. Glazing was 10 thou. Overlay of 10 thou strip was stuck round each outside frame; sills below panelling 40 thou × 1 mm. Ends were also two layers, left bare of planking at Luton end where chimney locates. At other end, door was two layers of 20 thou with 10 thou glazing and was stuck behind top layer. Frame round door made as for windows. Four sides were assembled round 40 thou floor. Interior seats (20 thou) and stove (Airfix mast) were fitted before flat roof of 40 thou was glued in position.

Model was then stuck to 80 thou base and 40 thou plinth laid on. The cornice and modillons were 20 thou; the latter were made from strips 2 mm wide, sanded to shape. Parapet was 40 thou. The chimney, scribed for brickwork, was built from 60 thou ends and 40 thou sides; London end located onto roof, Luton end went right down to base.

Painting: window frames—white. First four planks, outer window framing, door and doorframing—maroon; top planks to cornice and modillons—cream; base, plinth, parapet and roof—dark grey; chimney—brown-red.

Loco Sheds and Water Towers

St. Leonards, West Marina, was one of the larger Brighton sheds; it stood to the north of the coast line to Hastings opposite the now closed West Marina station. Badly damaged by enemy action during the last war, the roof had to be completely rebuilt; the new roof was similar to that at Templecombe. I worked to a drawing dated April, 1898 and the plans included here have been scaled up from this. On a drawing dated 1948, the thirteen bays were still extant, though the office lean-to building now came to within one bay of the west (Bexhill) end. From an H. C. Casserley photograph of 1931, it would appear that this office block already had been extended westwards: I do not know when the extension was built or, whether as quite often happens, the contract drawing was not adhered to and the block always covered this area. The 1898 drawing showed that the block contained, from west to east: Fitters' Shop, Stores, Cleaners, Drivers, Stores and Office. To return to the 1931 photograph: it shows that the jacks at that date were much shorter than on the drawing.

The northern lights are rather unusual in that they were vertical rather than sloping backward as normally found. Though St. Leonards was an L.B.S.C.R. shed, after the grouping S.E.C.R. locos invaded this territory, their shed at Hastings being closed. The distance from Hastings station involved a great deal of light engine working through the maze of tunnels and over Bo-Peep Junction. The heyday of the shed was before and just after the last war when the Schools Class predominated. My husband was brought up in a railway house overlooking the shed and his boyhood memories are full of these magnificent locos and the delight he had in them. I must say that in all my photographs of the shed after grouping there is not one Brighton loco in evidence! But today St. Leonards stands as forlorn and decrepit as the station opposite.

The model was built mainly from 60 thou for strength: with such a length of wall, the fear of warping could not be ruled out. There were thirteen bays in all, two being omitted from the accompanying drawing owing to lack of space. Each side wall was constructed from two layers of 60 thou, the top layer having the panel cut-outs removed from each bay. The top layer was scribed for bricks except where the lean-to buildings came; the lower layer was scribed on the panels except as above.

34

As the walls were so long, a join was necessary and this was made at the fifth bay, the join being hidden by the overlay. These overlays were 60 thou, scribed for bricks. Note that the overlay at the rear (west) end was shorter than remainder. The two layers of bricks at top and bottom of each panel were 20 thou scribed for bricks.

The front (east) elevation was made next. The brick part was again two layers of 60 thou, the height of this section being 66 mm. The upper half was built from 40 thou, the planks being scribed on; note that the two outer frames were left plain. Thirteen of these panels were required and I made them all at one go, marking them out in batches. The actual window frames were 20 thou, 1 mm shorter at each end than top 40 thou frame. They were stuck to the prepared 40 thou and then onto 10 thou glazing and left to dry under pressure overnight. The 20 thou strip along the top of each frame was glued on; at the front there were two additional strips beneath the windows, the lower 30 thou and the shorter top one 20 thou.

When the sides and glazed sections were dry, they were assembled. This took time as it was important to make sure that each bay had stuck squarely before adding the next. The usual gambit of assembling the sides round the floor could not be essayed. After all thirteen bays had set, the overlays at front and rear were added and the brickwork carried across the joins.

The thirteen roofs were made from 40 thou, scribed for slates. (The post-war rebuilding utilised corrugated sheeting.) The thirteenth roof has an extra length which forms a canopy over the rear doors. Valances for this canopy were 30 thou, suitably scribed; the rear beam across from the valances was 40 thou.

Fifty two jacks were made from 20 thou, four pieces to each jack. The ornamental strip round the top was 20 thou × 1 mm. The jacks were stuck down and 10 thou flashing added. Household pins, cut to size and secured in each corner with Evostik, formed the four cowl supports. Cowls were 20 thou, drawn out in one piece, each division cut half-through, then the piece was bound round a broom handle with string, immersed first in boiling then in cold water. Each cowl was then broken off in turn and glued onto the supports with Evostik.

The lean-to buildings were constructed from two layers of 40 thou, scribed for bricks. Window and door apertures were removed, window apertures on lower layer being 1 mm wider all round. Doors were scribed on lower layer; note that panelling was different on urinals building. Window frames were 10 thou, the bars being scribed on the 10 thou glazing. Windows at both ends were modelled in open positions. Ventilator on rear of urinals building was scribed deeply and widely to represent slits. Partitions were fitted between various departments in long lean-to when the building had been assembled round floor and to shed. Roofs were 30 thou, scribed for slates. Chimneys were built up from 40 thou, scribed for bricks; chimney tops

Loco shed

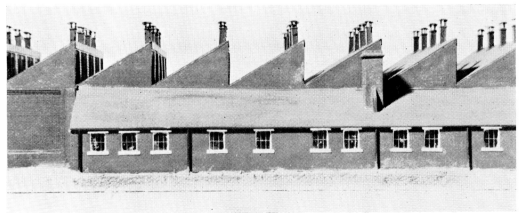

Eastbourne loco shed   C2 527 on turntable

were built up with 30 thou strips. Flashing was 10 thou.

Windowsills were 20 thou at top, 30 thou below; steps to lean-tos three layers of 40 thou. Drainpipes on shed were formed from metal knitting needles, bent over at the top to curve round overlays to gutters at base of each roof; lean-to drainpipes cut from cocktail sticks.

Shed doors were 40 thou, scribed on both sides; overlays and hinges were cut from 10 thou. Posts were built from 40 thou. The doors were modelled in the open position.

Painting: Brickwork—dark red. Doors, framing of north lights and drainpipes—Southern Railway green. Inner frames of north lights, sills, vent at rear of urinals, bargeboards, and valances—cream. Jacks and roofs—dark grey. Cowls—black. North lights and chimneys were dirtied with anthracite soot.

Eastbourne shed was, until 1912, of the roundhouse type rarely encountered in this country. The L.B.S.C.R. also built roundhouses at Battersea and Horsham, the latter similar to Eastbourne but having more roads. I have included a photograph of my model as a contrast to the more orthodox sheds described. The shed at Horsham was still standing when I was there in January, 1969, but in very dilapidated condition.

Glyn Neath, G.W.R. I built this shed for Edward Russell of Footscray, Australia, from his own excellent drawings and photographs as a thank you for the period cars he had sent to fill up Eastbourne's roads. It was constructed from the usual materials and thicknesses, the large columns bearing the water tank being plastic knitting needles. The worst part to make was the top of the tank with its awkward curve-under and this was a singular failure; not only did it look wrong but during the long sea passage, it collapsed! Mr. Russell himself then made a much more durable and successful top. A photograph of the prototype by B. K. B. Green was published in *Railway World* for November 1955.

Littlehampton was, to my mind, the most attractive of the small L.B.S.C.R. sheds. It also provided a well-known and easily obtained setting for photographs of locos as it was near the platform. The shed did not close until 1938 when the coast line was electrified; but it was not demolished being incorporated into the new platform added when the station was rebuilt and appears to be used for parcels.

Glyn Neath loco shed

From the drawings it will be seen that several parts of the buildings differ in quite marked respects. On the contract drawing the shed windows were shown as being located in a lower position than on all photographs. The tank was depicted without a top or diagonal bracing; this bracing was typical of many L.B.S.C.R. tanks. And the chimney had a different top. In earlier photographs a ladder was shown against the tank on the station side; it was definitely there in 1927, but later it had disappeared. Brick arrangement beneath tank differs in photographs to that on plan, see alternative side elevation. Doors at front shown on drawings as opening inwards whereas on all photographs they open outwards.

On coming to build the model careful note was taken of the thickness of the main walls. Without overlays these were 4 mm thick. I decided to scribe the inside walls as well; normally I do not bother but with large door openings and a relatively small surface to be scribed, the extra chore was worthwhile. There were seven layers to each wall: top overlay; second had arch over windows and panel cut away beneath; third had brick panel beneath windows; fourth and fifth plain except for window apertures; sixth scribed and with arch over windows; seventh the same as top except that it was 6 mm narrower at each end. Sides narrow from 210 mm–198 mm over the seven layers. When all the walls had been prepared, plain 5 thou glazing was inserted between fourth and fifth layers and all the layers glued together and left to dry under pressure for two days.

Front wall of shed was also seven layers thick, each layer 1 mm narrower at each end. First five layers had door apertures of same width, but last two were 1 mm narrower at either side to allow doors to be fitted; the doors were to open inwards as shown on plan. When front and side walls were finished, they were glued together, front fitting between sides.

The rear wall of the shed was five layers thick. The door was not shown in elevation on drawing, so I copied the design from Epsom shed. Rear wall was scribed as it was plainly visible, and door aperture removed. The door was located on the third layer and was panelled with 10 thou. Transom aperture was removed on all five layers. Fifth layer formed *front* wall of water tower and was 72 mm and 85 mm high—the higher part was scribed as it would be seen above shed roof. This upper section was "stepped" in reverse to the lower part, i.e. each layer was 2 mm *narrower* from front to rear while lower part was 2 mm *wider*.

Side walls of the water tower were 5 mm thick. Station side had a door, road side a window; the window was same shape and size as those on shed. Door was recessed 3 mm; double arch was scribed over door aperture on second and third layers; door panelling was cut from 10 thou.

The rear wall was also 5 mm thick. Windows were same size as on shed. When wall was scribed the part where the chimney stood was left blank. Extra layers of bricks round top of water tower were formed from 40 thou; on actual shed,

37

Littlehampton Loco shed—rail elevation

Front elevation

of 40 thou was fitted, each piece 1 mm shorter at each end. The actual chimney was tapered and made from one layer of scribed 40 thou. Two parts were glued together and left overnight; when dry, brickwork was carried over joins and whole structure was cemented in place. Top was built up from 30 thou strips with a liberal amount of glue. Plinths were fitted

End elevation

30 thou was used for these layers and for the overlays by the windows. Sills were also 30 thou. Glazing was stuck *behind* window apertures on water tower to give proper depth. All window frames were cut individually from 10 thou with a sharp no. 1 blade. Two were required per window on the shed, outside and inside; water tower windows had outside frames only.

Chimney base was 40 thou, scribed for bricks, back piece left blank; an inner layer

round shed, water tower and chimney, tops being angled back 1 mm.

The tank was made from 40 thou, the four sides being assembled round a 40 thou floor. When this had set, it was glued to a further 80 thou base. This base was sanded to form a turn-under. Tank was now stuck to 40 thou false flat roof of water tower. Strips of 10 thou × 1 mm were positioned for rivetted joints; roundels were made by leather punch and the diagonals were scribed on.

Shed was now coated with dark red plastic paint, inside and out. The windows were carefully painted a stone colour and doors brown.

Shed doors were made from 40 thou, scribed on both sides for planking. Overlays were cut from 10 thou in one piece; these were painted brown, the rest of the doors being stone. Steps to water tower entrance were built up from 40 thou and painted stone.

Roof of shed was built as an experiment. The main roof was 40 thou, scribed for slates, the four pieces being cemented into position round the open well which would receive upper, glazed section, and onto 40 thou strips which had been stuck to top of walls to form eaves. The slatted sides of this section had a framework of 30 thou, strips of 20 thou being glued behind.

The ends of this section were cut from 40 thou, scribed for planks both sides; overlays of 10 and 20 thou being added.

Underneath view

The ends were stuck in place on main roof and left to set overnight. The slatted sides were cemented outside the ends and to the main roof. Top of this upper part was glazed; a 20 thou frame was prepared and 5 thou glazing glued behind it, this being scribed on. When dry, it was stuck to side and ends. The top roof was two 20 thou strips cemented together and to ends. Bevelled 40 thou strips were glued at the ends of both roofs. 1 mm square strips 8 mm long were fitted across top of well between glazed sections to coincide with 20 thou glazing bars to give extra strength to this section. These strips can be seen on the photograph showing inside the shed.

Tank ends were marked out round 10″ gramophone record and cut to shape with scissors, afterwards sanding smooth. They were stuck in place and when set a 20 thou sheet which had been warmed and curved by the electric fire was glued over ends and to tank sides.

Roof of shed, tank and tank roof were painted dark grey. Glazed roof of shed was painted stone.

Finally drainpipes of wire were fitted with split pins which located into no. 68 holes drilled through shed walls to represent clamps; wire was bent to shape and top located into hole drilled in eaves. Drainpipes were then painted brown.

Radlett water tower stood by the up slow platform at the London end of the station. It was always a favourite of mine as it seemed to represent a great deal of what was good on the old Midland Railway line and I have never been reconciled to its razing. So when the H.M.R.S. wanted some models for the Bedford–St. Pancras Extension Centenary Exhibition, I immediately suggested building the water tower. The idea having been accepted, I turned to the drawings I possessed in Beal's *Modelling the Old Time Railways* and in the *Model Railway Constructor* for April 1957, the article and drawing in the latter being the work of Malcolm Cross. The model was built from an amalgam of the two drawings.

The main building was built first; sides and ends were each three layers of 40 thou; rear layer had door planking scribed on. Sides and ends were scribed for bricks. Arches were formed by scribing with old pair of dividers, cracking out curve and then cleaning up; bricks round arches were scribed with no. 3 blade, as were those round windows. Strengthening piece taken from top layer door aperture was cemented behind actual doors to prevent warping. Ends fitted between sides. The ventilating grilles were scribed diagonally on second layer, aperture being cut from top layer and a frame 1 mm wide all round partially cut through. The window at the London end was bricked up at some time in the tower's history and this was scribed on third layer. Scribed overlays round windows were made from 40 thou, those at right angles to the windows being glued in first, with those which fitted parallel to the windows cemented on top. A strip of 20 thou × 2 mm to form cornice was glued at top of overlays. Keystones were 40 thou, sanded to shape. Window frames were cut from 10 thou, the bars being scribed on the 10 thou glazing; semi-circular bars were scribed on with dividers.

Smaller building was made in same way, again being 3 mm thick to prevent any chance of warping. Overlays halfway up walls were built up from 20 thou. 40 thou flat roofs and floors were fitted to both buildings, the floor of the main building

Radlett water tower: rear elevation

Radlett Water Tower

being painted grey as with almost ground level windows, a white floor would have been very noticeable.

The tank was two layers of 10 thou and one of 20 thou. The lowest (20 thou) was left plain; the two top layers were cut out for panels and rivetting. Centres of cut-away panels were used for raised parts, which saved wastage—note curved corners of these panels. When the sides had set round a 40 thou floor, I fitted a second floor for strength, and later, when the tank showed a tendency to warp, put a 40 thou flat roof on tank: nobody seemed to know what actually should have been there and it looked better than warped sides. An inspection hatch was scribed on this roof. A water gauge was made from an Airfix sprue, the pulley from scrap and the filler pipe from biro tube heated over the gas stove and then bent to shape. Safety rails at the top of the ladder came from a Rocket kit but proved too flimsy under exhibition wear and tear. A ladder was fixed in position but had been removed by the time the photographs had been taken.

Cornices under tank and above flat roof on subsidiary building were built up from various thicknesses of styrene strip.

The tank and roofs were painted dark grey; all brickwork was dark red; cornices, mouldings, keystones, parapets, cream poster paint; grilles, black; window frames were left white; and doors were painted maroon.

The whole model was liberally dirtied with anthracite soot applied with index finger. It has now found a home on Terry Jenkins' layout in Luton.

Goods Sheds

The rather massive shed at **Littlehampton,** which contrasts with the comparatively small loco shed, is of the two-storeyed type also found at Tunbridge Wells West, Arundel and Seaford, though Tunbridge Wells West at least has an entirely different roof arrangement.

Five layers of 40 thou were required for the sides. The top layer was drawn out on separate pieces and then fitted together on top of second layer to avoid wastage. From drawing it will be noted that the two sides do not correspond on the centre section, the road side having a gable and door for upper storey, while the rail elevation is entirely windows. There are also doors on the road side for access to ground floor. On the rail side the top layer central overlays are 17 mm wide instead of the regular 12 mm.

The rail elevation was built first. Bricks were scribed on top layer pieces; second layer was 1 mm shorter at each end, the arches scribed over the windows and the window apertures and panels below removed, the remaining parts of this layer

41

which would show were then scribed for bricks. Third layer was a further 1 mm shorter each end and only window apertures removed, the exposed panels being scribed for bricks. The fourth and fifth layers were correspondingly shortened and only the window apertures removed. All five layers were stuck together and left to dry for a day.

On the road side the top layer was again laid out in separate pieces, apart from the gable section which was made all in one piece. Second layer had large semi-circular aperture on gable above door; the main door apertures were also removed; window arches scribed on and layer treated as third layer on rail side; fourth layer had window apertures removed but all door planking scribed on. Fifth layer as on rail side.

Ends: These were again constructed of five layers. Top layer had triangular cut-out on gable, as had second and third layers, the triangle on each succeeding layer 1 mm narrower all round. Fourth layer had bricks scribed on bared triangular section; fifth was plain. Top layer had arch scribed over doorway and aperture 40 mm wide; aperture on second layer same width, but on third-fifth layers aperture was 38 mm wide as doors open outwards. At south end, wall was left blank of scribing where office would come, but on layers one, two, four and five inner door aperture was removed and on all five layers window was cut out; the glazing was set between layers three and four. Door panelling was on both sides of third layer and cut from 10 thou. Recessed panels with rounded tops were the same at both ends: first layer had rectangular panels round arched panels removed; second layer minus arched panels; third layer had brickwork in panels; fourth and fifth layers plain. N.B. Doors

Littlehampton goods warehouse—end elevation

Goods warehouse—road elevation

on north end are located on opposite side to those on south elevation.

End doors were made from 40 thou, being the cut-outs from the top layer, scribed for planking on both sides. Framing and overlays on all doors were cut from 10 thou. End doors were glued in the open position.

Windows: thirty four semi-circular windows were required. Design was drawn out on card in Indian ink. A sheet of 10 thou glazing was placed over this design and the bars were scribed on with dividers. This was a ruse I had already tried when building Henlow station which had sported the ornate Midland Railway window frames. Scribing marks were filled with stone-coloured paint and glazing rubbed clean.

Office walls were made 3 mm thick, the top layer being scribed for bricks. The door was recessed 2 mm and its panelling was cut from 10 thou. 40 thou floor was fitted at ground level and the actual floor which located on 40 thou formers 16 mm high. When windows had been glued behind top layer, flat roof was put in. Roof itself was 30 thou, scribed for slates; ridging was 10 thou. Windowsills were 1 mm square, 1 mm longer than apertures each end. Steps were built up from 40 thou, each step 3 mm higher than next; 20 thou top to every step was added with $\frac{1}{2}$ mm overhang.

The shed roof was made from 40 thou, scribed for slates and the west side (road) cut out round gable. Gable roof was

30 thou scribed for slates. Ridging was 10 thou, 2 mm wide. Chimney was built from 40 thou, scribed for bricks; top made from two layers of 30 thou. Flashing 10 thou.

Platform inside shed was made from 40 thou on 40 thou formers 16 mm high. End legs cut from 40 thou. Section taken out from platform to receive steps which were built up from 40 thou. Part of platform was removed where centre doors opened inwards.

Painting: all outside and inside walls of shed and office painted dark red. Roofs were dark grey. Framing and overlays on doors, brown. Planking on doors, windowsills and steps, stone.

Eastbourne goods shed was modelled in low relief as the site available on the layout was not sufficiently large to permit the shed to be modelled in full.

Sides were made from four layers of 40 thou. Panels containing windows cut

Rail elevation

43

from top two layers, first layer being scribed for bricks. Third layer had window apertures and rectangular panel below removed; fourth layer had aperture cut out for windows. See side elevation. Arches scribed out and cut from 30 thou, stuck in position and overlay of same thickness glued at base of these arches. Moulding layers at top of sides various widths of 20 thou. Window frames were cut from 10 thou with a sharp no. 1 blade, but the finished effect was too heavy and if I built it again, I would use the method described for Littlehampton. Glazing 10 thou, glued behind frames.

End was also five layers of 40 thou, again see drawing for break-down. Note that the flanking panels are not symmetrical. Support girder over doorway was 40 thou, with a 20 thou strip 2 mm wide at bottom. Cornice on gable 20 thou. Flat roof was 40 thou fitted just above line of girder.

Roof was 30 thou, scribed for slates, the glazed section cut out. A second layer of the same thickness was glued behind, the skylight aperture 2 mm wider all round to allow skylight to be located behind first roof layer. This skylight was made from 10 thou, cut out in one piece (where I did not slice through glazing bars by mistake!). It was backed by 10 thou glazing and the finished section cemented in place.

The shed was painted the same yellow brick colour as the station and signal cabin. Arches round windows were stone as were mouldings and cornice. Skylight frame and bars, buff. Roof was dark grey.

Signal Cabins

Littlehampton. I am including a drawing of this, though at the time of writing I have yet to build it myself. The style is very much like that of boxes on the South London Line. I cannot vouchsafe the accuracy of this drawing, as I calculated it from the ground measurements on a 40′ to 1″ plan and from a colour slide taken at an oblique angle, kindly loaned to me by Peter Barker of Copenhagen. The brickwork is dull red; the windows on the ground floor are now bricked up.

Fittleworth. From the one photograph of this signal cabin which I own, it looked a typical L.B.S.C.R. brickbuilt cabin, so I built it to the drawing published in the *Model Railway News* for February 1954.

40 thou was used for the walls. Brickwork was scribed on the lower half below window level except at the back where it was continued to the eaves. The apertures for the upper frames had to be cut carefully as it was easier to snap the corner frames which were supposed to remain intact than to remove the styrene sheet in between. All window and door apertures were removed and planking on upper part of cabin scribed. A 40 thou second layer was next cut for each wall; the rear one went up to the eaves, the two sides formed L-shapes as the planked sections had to be backed, while the remaining part came up to within 1 mm of the sliding frames. Both doors were scribed for planking on lower layer.

When the four walls had been prepared with appropriate backing, they were assembled round a 40 thou ground floor. The lower window frames were cut from 10 thou, stuck to 10 thou glazing and glued behind apertures; windows in rear wall were made the same way. Sills were 20 thou × 1 mm. A 40 thou plinth, scribed for bricks, was added, the top being angled back. The board from which the firebuckets depended was cut from 20 thou and the buckets made from plastic sprues. This completed the bottom half.

A 40 thou floor was fitted at the correct height and while it was setting, attention was turned to the windows. Frames were 20 thou, cemented to 10 thou glazing which was then scribed for bars. These bars were filled with white poster paint and the glazing rubbed clean. A dab of

Fittleworth

Fittleworth

white paint in each upper corner gave the characteristic Brighton curve to the tops of the windows. The frames were then carefully fitted into place.

The lever frame was made from two layers of 60 thou, sanded to shape; levers were formed from household pins, cut to length and burned in. A Tri-ang fireman was placed behind the frame, minus his shovel. Desk was made from scraps of styrene; the stove and its flue were fashioned from Airfix sailing ship masts. A flat roof of 40 thou was now fitted to keep the cabin square. A further flat roof made from 30 thou was stuck on top, with an overhang which formed eaves. Roof brackets were 20 thou. Roof was four pieces of 30 thou, scribed for slates. Exterior stovepipe was made from cocktail sticks. Flashing was 10 thou.

The sloping sill below the cabin windows was cut from 40 thou, the ends dovetailing together on the angle. Next made was the platform, from 40 thou scribed for planking, to which were added stairs from an Airfix signal cabin kit. Balustrades and banisters were 20 thou, each cut out in one piece.

Painting: Doors, outer framing, banisters, balustrades, roof brackets, and sills were Southern Railway green. Planking was cream, platform and stairs were brown, roof and stovepipe dark grey, fire buckets were red. All brickwork was painted a warm red, then suitably weathered with soot.

Eastbourne cabin is the largest I have attempted so far. The drawing appended here was again calculated, this time from the known outside dimensions at ground level and the height of the box. These had been measured for me by Ron Hodges of Polegate. The remaining dimensions were worked out from photographs.

Four layers of 40 thou formed each wall. First and second layers were cut out to reveal panels; top layer was scribed, but second layer only scribed where it formed plinth. Third layer had window and door apertures removed, care being taken with the pointed tops and then was scribed where necessary. Fourth layer was plain on three walls; on the fourth the door planking was scribed on. The completed walls were assembled round a 40 thou floor and when window frames and bars had been cut from 10 thou, with 10 thou glazing stuck behind, and cemented in place, a flat 40 thou roof was fitted. The final construction on the lower part was the making of remaining plinths from 40 thou, scribed for bricks.

The shell of the upper storey was again 40 thou, scribed for planking, and when door and window apertures had been cut out, it was glued to a second layer which came to within 1 mm of windows. All framing was 20 thou and two 20 thou layers formed the door, backed by 10 thou glazing. The longest and most difficult job was cutting out the many window frames from 10 thou: a sharp no. 1 blade was essential. Each section was made separately and stuck to 10 thou glazing after it had been painted buff. The drawing shows which windows fit in front and which behind. I modelled several in the open position. The walls were assembled round a 40 thou base which was then stuck to the flat roof of the lower part. The actual floor of the cabin, again 40 thou, was fitted next and the interior detailed as already described for Fittleworth, except that two signalmen were required for so large a box.

A 40 thou flat roof was cemented in position, followed by another with an overhang of 7 mm all round. Brackets were shaped up from 30 thou and stuck under eaves and also under overhang of lower section. The roof was made from four pieces of 30 thou, scribed for slates; ridging was 10 thou. The exterior stovepipe and the two vents on the ridge were biro

Eastbourne—signal cabin

tubing; stovepipe support was wire, while the cowls on the vents were 20 thou discs.

The platform was made from two pieces of 40 thou held apart by a strip of 20 thou × 3 mm on three sides; the top was scribed for planks. When this empty sandwich was in position, railings and banisters of 20 thou were added, the posts having extra layers of 10 thou strips on each side. Stairs were laid individually between 20 thou sides. The vertical supports were cut from bullhead rail.

Drainpipes were fashioned from plastic-covered bellwire but were not too successful as the supposedly straight parts show a tendency to kink.

Painting: all brickwork except round the windows and door was plough yellow brick, the fancy brickwork being red—I have shown these red parts on the drawing. Framing, banisters, railings, platform, doors, eaves and drainpipes—umber. Planking and window frames were buff, while the roof, stovepipe and vents were medium grey.

Glyn Neath. I built this for Edward Russell of Footscray, Australia, at the same time the loco shed was made and again to his own excellent drawings. It was my first G.W.R. cabin and I believe typical of this company's cabins with the engineers' blue bricks at corners and round windows. The model was constructed in the same manner as the foregoing Southern cabins, with obvious detail differences. I despatched it in two halves so that the interior could be detailed in true G.W.R. fashion as I did not know the number of levers, etc. The

two vents on the ridge were made from biro "nibs" burned into the ridge. I would point out that the model *does* stand straight—we tried photographing it on a brown paper base with wobbly results.

Claygate. This model was built to a drawing in the *Railway Modeller* for April, 1968 and which was also repeated when my article appeared in June 1969.

As usual the brick base was built of two layers of 40 thou; a third layer was added for the raised overlays, leaving a gap at the front for the point rodding. The ground floor door was scribed on the third layer. A plinth of 30 thou was scribed for bricks and stuck on, angled back at the top. A false floor was fitted at plinth level and a flat roof.

Glyn Neath

Glyn Neath

The upper half was again of 40 thou, the planking scribed on, noting that the planking on the rear wall was different. The four sides were assembled round a 40 thou base. Window frames were cut from 20 thou, with 10 thou glazing on which the bars were scribed; the two centre windows were set in front of the side ones as the latter slide open. Upper windows were made the same way, but all set in an equal amount. The two centre top front windows were covered at the back with white poster paint. A ledge 30 thou × 1 mm was stuck below the windows round three sides of the cabin. When the top and bottom halves of the cabin had been joined, a 1 mm × 2 mm strip was set on the brickwork right round the cabin and slightly bevelled. The 40 thou floor was now added, together with a lever frame shaped up from two layers of 60 thou and levers made from household pins burned into the frame and cut to length. When the signalman had been positioned before the frame, a flat roof of 40 thou was fitted in place.

The roof was four pieces of 30 thou, scribed for slates; ridging was 20 thou strip; stovepipe was biro tubing. Guttering was cut from 10 thou and eaves from 20 thou. The entrance porch was built from 30 thou, the planking scribed on; window frames were 20 thou fitting *into* aperture and not as usual behind it. The platform was 20 thou, scribed for planking, its supports being shaped from 40 thou. The balustrade, banisters and steps were cut from 20 thou; the latter were fiddly and had to be watched carefully while drying to prevent them slipping out of alignment. Drainpipes were shaped from wire.

Painting: brickwork, dark red; all framing, balustrading, banisters, drainpipes, and guttering, Humbrol no. 3 green; planking, platform supports and eaves, cream; roofs, stovepipe, platform and steps, dark grey. A 30 thou base was provided and painted brownish-yellow to highlight the colours on the model. The last touch was added by typing the box name on card and having trimmed it to shape, fixing it in place with Evostik.

Claygate box

Other Railway Buildings

The prototype of the railway cottages shown in the drawings on p. 65 were built to fit into a site beside the level crossing on Stockbridge Road, Chichester. Many ancillary railway buildings in the Chichester area were faced with flints and it appeared from the original drawings and personal observation from a train that this material had been employed on the cottages. However, a pre-war photograph which came into my possession recently shows a brick facing, but by then it was too late as the model had been finished as shown on the drawings.

A start was made on the front (west) elevation. 40 thou styrene was used throughout for both outer and inner walls. Having cut out window and door apertures (including the blind ones on the first floor), I scribed out the corner bricks and those over the ground floor windows. The bricked up windows were scribed on the inner layer. I flooded the surface of the outer wall with cement and made flint-like whorls with a small screwdriver. This soon dried and the two layers were glued together. The rear wall was made in the same way, extra scribing being needed down the line of the party wall. Note the various decorative touches round the windows—no standardisation in those days! Lastly the north and south walls were prepared, the latter extended to form the end wall of the lean-to building.

When thoroughly dry, the four walls were assembled round a 40 thou base. Window frames were built up from two layers of 10 thou, the outer painted green, the inner left white. Glazing was 10 thou with bars scribed on. When the windows were in place, the front doors were made from 20 thou, with the panelling cut from the top layer; doorframing was built up from various thicknesses and, like the doors, painted green. The ground and first floors and flat roof were cemented in position and left to dry out thoroughly.

The lean-to building was made from 40 thou and stuck firmly in place, on the south wall; the two doors were scribed on the top layer and 10 thou framing added. There are nine layers of hanging tiles on this wall; these were cut in strips from 10 thou, each row overlapping 1 mm and working upwards; the vertical cuts were placed alternately.

Windowsills were made from 20 thou strips.

The main roofs are not identical and care was taken, when cutting the 30 thou from which they were made, to get the dimensions correct. Chimneys were made from 40 thou, scribed for bricks, and set in position. The tiling was now laid on, as described for Rotherfield. The corner tiles were punched out from 10 thou with an office punch, cut in half and laid on one by one, again working from the eaves upwards.

The rear wall enclosing the area was constructed from three layers of 40 thou,

Cottages at Chichester on Eastbourne layout

scribed for bricks where it would show above ground level. The top is sanded round and brickwork scribed on. Lean-to roofs were 30 thou, the chimney on the rear one made from 40 thou and stuck on before the tiling was added. The remaining short wall on the north side was again made from three layers of 40 thou, scribed and rounded. An area floor was cemented in and then the two flights of steps, built up from 40 thou. Drainpipes were knitting needles and painted green. Lastly the cornices and modillons were made from 20 thou and well stuck on.

Now the entire building apart from the brick parts was given a coat of G.W.R. freight stock grey, the idea being that flints always seem to stand out from a dark background. All brickwork was painted a deep red. Finally the flint walls were coated with white poster paint which of course did not cover properly and so formed the "pepper and salt" appearance characteristic of this finish.

A short pavement was added at the front, the gratings above the lower floor windows being scribed and then painted green while the pavement itself was dark grey.

Pocklington station was on the N.E.R. line between York and Market Weighton. The model to be described is, as stated on the plan dated January 31, 1894, a cottage and two stall stable converted from a warehouse.

Difficulty was experienced during the making of the 4 mm drawing because the length of Elevation to Road and to Rail differed on the original plan by a matter of 26 mm which is quite a lot. Having consulted the ground plan, I realised that Elevation to Rails was correct. What I think happened was that the draughtsman took the side elevation measurements in error for the Road Elevation. I made Road and Rail the same length otherwise it throws the entire building completely. I modelled it in brick which I hope is correct— no doubt it will prove to have been stone-built. Before embarking on the brickwork, however, I dug out some photographs of Nunburnholme and Londesborough on the same line and these stations were brick-

Cottages at Chichester

built—I therefore assumed Pocklington to have been likewise.

The model. Walls were made from two layers of 40 thou, doors being scribed on the lower layer and 10 thou panelling added. Where windows had been bricked up, they were scribed with remainder of wall, then cut out and replaced upside down to allow for the slight misalignment often noticed in bricking-up. Window frames were 20 thou and look too heavy; 10 thou would have been better. Sills were 30 thou as was the roof which was scribed for slates; 10 thou ridging was laid on and the bargeboards cut from 20 thou.

The manure pit. On the original plan this was 30 mm (7′ 6″) across. On a revised plan (7th March, 1894) stapled to the original, this had been extended to 54 mm (13′ 6″). I modelled it as shown on original plan, making the walls from three layers of 40 thou, scribed for bricks, on both outer layers. Capping was cut from 20 thou, scribed for stones.

Inner walls of yard were scribed as well as outer as they show; note the shape of the yard. Doors of outbuildings were scribed on top layer of 40 thou. Outbuilding roofs were 30 thou, scribed for slates. All steps were built from 40 thou.

Chimneys on main building were made from 40 thou, scribed for bricks; 10 thou flashing and moulding round tops was glued on. Drainpipes were plastic-covered bellwire stuck on with Evostik.

Brickwork was painted dark red; all woodwork was N.E.R. chocolate; roofs

Cottages at Pocklington

were medium grey; yard was dark grey; sills were left unpainted but suitably dirtied.

The completed model was glued to an 80 thou base which was then painted the same dark grey as the yard.

Conclusion

In the foregoing pages I have tried to give some idea of how I work, of the satisfaction to be gained from prototype modelling and the results obtained from polystyrene as a modelling medium. By admitting errors I hope to save others from the same pitfalls, though this is in no way to suggest that my methods could not be improved upon. With each successive model I find new ways of solving problems in constructing buildings: indeed, in this lies half the pleasure, for if it were possible to reach the ultimate in modelling there would be no fun left, no fresh fields to conquer, and no more mistakes from which to learn.

I have also tried to show that an average modeller like myself can make models of actual structures and not be forced to purchase kits producing buildings exactly like those to be found on many other layouts. Of course, building from scratch takes considerably more time but the completed result is much more gratifying besides lending individuality to a layout. I must confess to a possibly absurd thrill when studying my "latest" and find myself wondering just how I managed to make it, yet I hope that faults are more glaring to me than to anyone else. As one's standards improve so must accuracy: an approximation is no longer satisfying. Towards the completion of a large model, when one is probably becoming a little tired of it and subconsciously seeking pastures new, it is tempting to think, for example, "Well, I'm not sure the chimney *actually* went there—if I don't put it in no-one will be the wiser." But next morning one sets to, and the offending chimney takes no more than fifteen minutes to make, photos and plans having again been studied to ensure that, as far as it is possible to know, it *is* in the right place.

So to me this question of buildings is important. However good the locos are, or even the rolling stock, set on their track among a hotch-potch of kits they irretrievably lose prototype atmosphere. And there is less excuse these days for making do, for at least one prototype building drawing is published each month in the model press. A desire to get things running need not prohibit the station from being a model of a prototype: the ground plan of the relevant buildings can be drawn out on the baseboard, and each building constructed can satisfyingly be "keyed" into place, giving the trains somewhere to stop while the station is under construction. Space problems posed by the prototype can be partially overcome by platform shortening while leaving the actual buildings correct. Architecturally quite elaborate stations like Petworth or Wokingham had comparatively short platforms, especially in pre-grouping days; many Southern stations have had their platforms lengthened in recent years to accommodate twelve-coach e.m.u.'s.

If this book encourages anyone to "have a go", as the current phrase invites, then I shall feel that my slow stumblings towards better models of railway buildings will have been immensely worthwhile. Scratch-building certainly isn't difficult—it just takes a little more time.

WORKING DRAWINGS

SCALE
2 mm = 1 foot

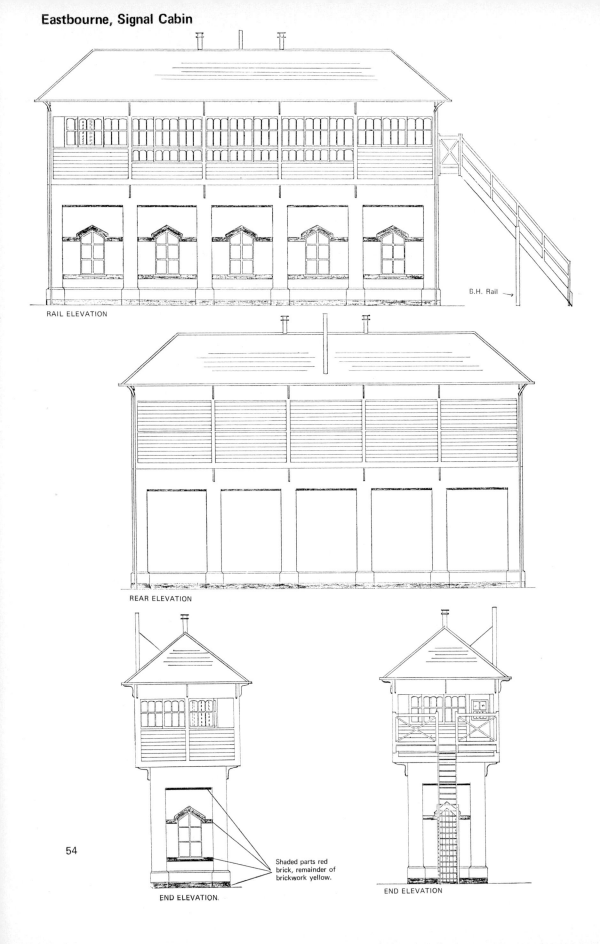

RAIL ELEVATION

B.H. Rail →

REAR ELEVATION

END ELEVATION.

Shaded parts red brick, remainder of brickwork yellow.

END ELEVATION

Eastbourne, Goods Shed

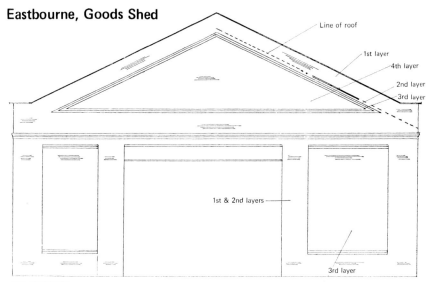

Line of roof

1st layer

4th layer

2nd layer

3rd layer

1st & 2nd layers

3rd layer

END ELEVATION

Goods Shed

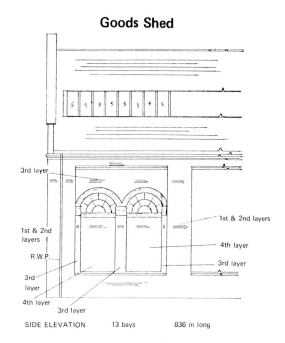

3rd layer

1st & 2nd layers

1st & 2nd layers

4th layer

R.W.P.

3rd layer

3rd layer

4th layer

3rd layer

SIDE ELEVATION   13 bays   836 m long

Wokingham

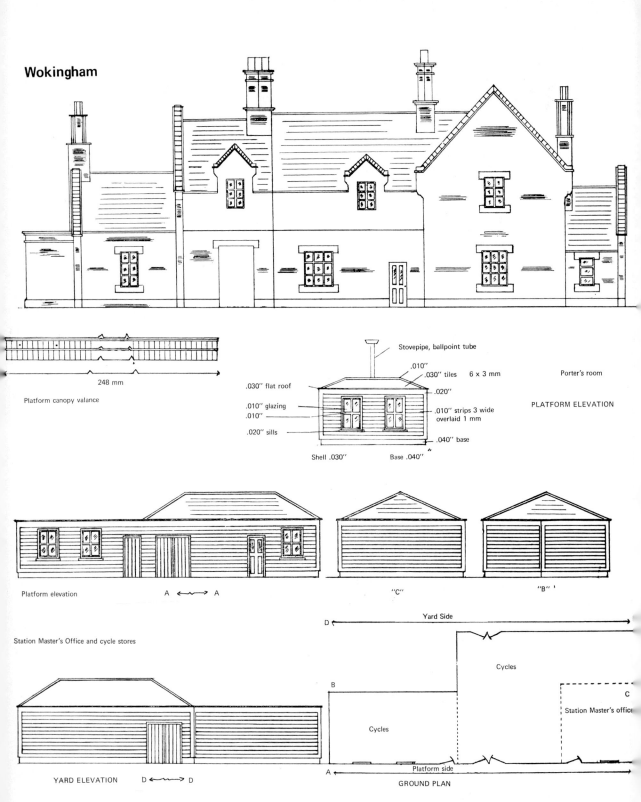

Platform canopy valance

248 mm

Stovepipe, ballpoint tube

.010"
.030" tiles   6 x 3 mm

Porter's room

.030" flat roof

.010" glazing
.010"

.020"

.010" strips 3 wide
overlaid 1 mm

.020" sills

.040" base

Shell .030"   Base .040"

PLATFORM ELEVATION

Platform elevation   A ←——→ A

"C"

"B"

Station Master's Office and cycle stores

YARD ELEVATION   D ←——→ D

Yard Side

D

Cycles

B

Cycles

C

Station Master's office

A

Platform side

GROUND PLAN

56

Wokingham

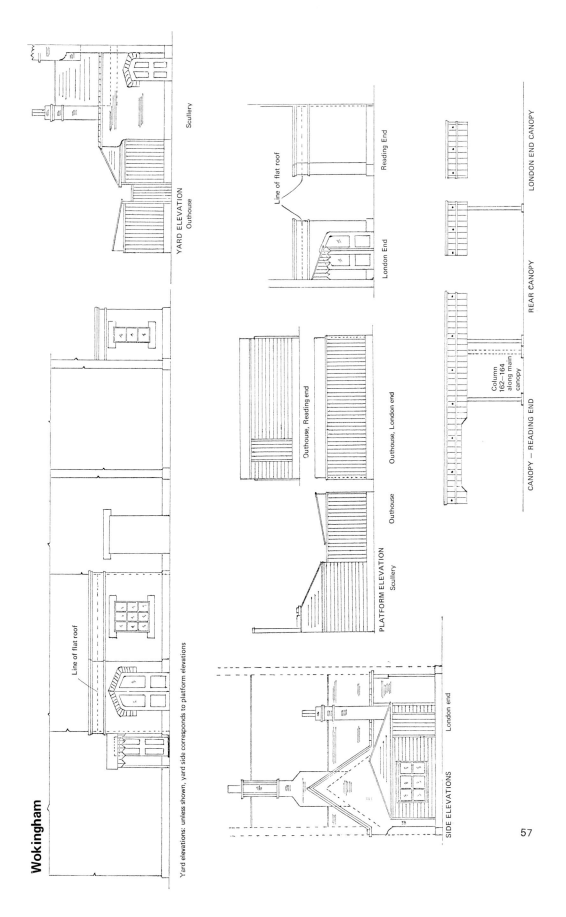

YARD ELEVATION
Outhouse   Scullery

Line of flat roof

Yard elevations: unless shown, yard side corresponds to platform elevations

Line of flat roof

Reading End

London End

PLATFORM ELEVATION
Scullery   Outhouse   Outhouse, London end   Outhouse, Reading end

SIDE ELEVATIONS
London end

LONDON END CANOPY

REAR CANOPY

Column 162–164 along main canopy

CANOPY – READING END

57

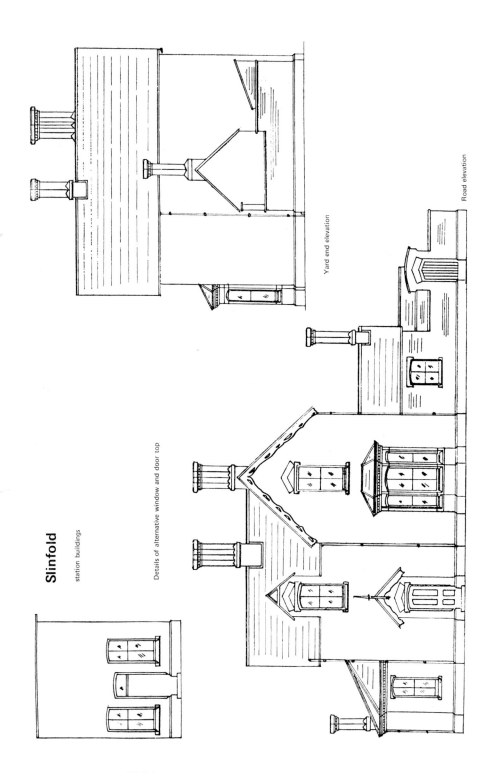

Slinfold

station buildings

Details of alternative window and door top

Yard end elevation

Road elevation

58

Slinfold

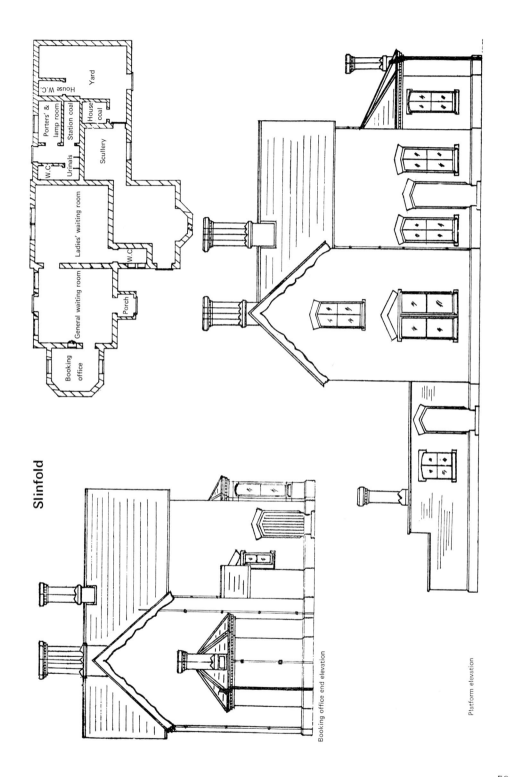

Booking office end elevation

Platform elevation

General waiting room

Ladies' waiting room

Booking office

Porch

W.C

W.C

Urinals

Porters' & lamp room

Station coal

House coal

Scullery

House W.C

Yard

59

Chichester, Down Side

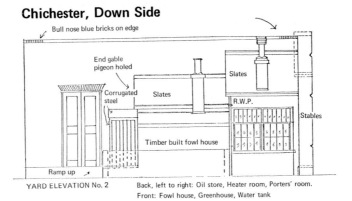

Bull nose blue bricks on edge

End gable pigeon holed

Corrugated steel

Slates

Slates

R.W.P.

Stables

Timber built fowl house

Ramp up

YARD ELEVATION No. 2   Back, left to right: Oil store, Heater room, Porters' room.
Front: Fowl house, Greenhouse, Water tank

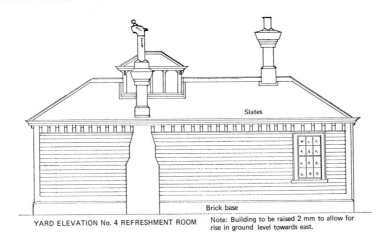

Vent

Slates

Refreshment room

Porters' room

Corrugated steel sheeting

Blue bricks on edge

Slates

YARD ELEVATION No. 3   Note: Refreshment room to be raised 2 mm to allow for rise in ground level towards east end of down platform.
Back: Stables. Front: Fodder store, Manure pit, R.R. coals

Slates

Brick base

YARD ELEVATION No. 4 REFRESHMENT ROOM   Note: Building to be raised 2 mm to allow for rise in ground level towards east.

Bull nose blue bricks on edge

Refreshment room

Blue bricks on edge

Ramp up

YARD ELEVATION NO. 5   Urinals for use on race days only

Chichester, Down Side

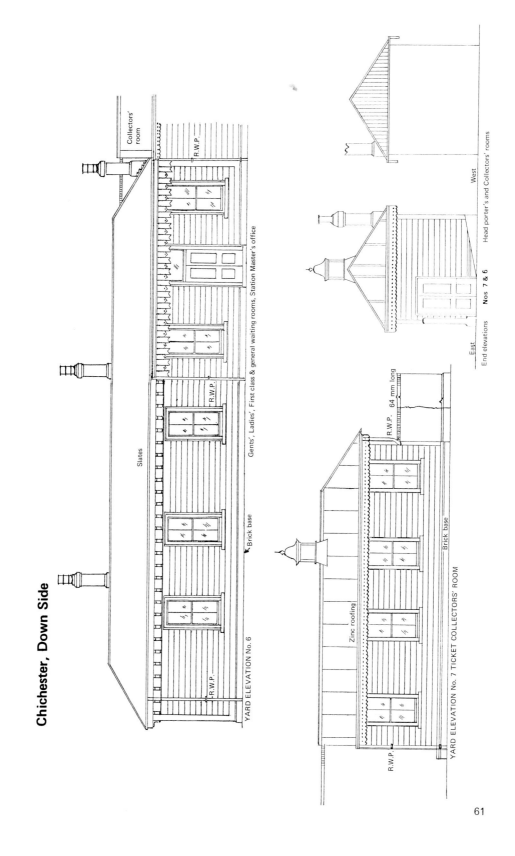

Collectors' room

R.W.P.

Slates

Gents', Ladies', First class & general waiting rooms, Station Master's office

R.W.P.

Brick base

YARD ELEVATION No. 6

West

Head porter's and Collectors' rooms

East

Nos 7 & 6

End elevations

R.W.P. 64 mm long

Zinc roofing

Brick base

R.W.P.

YARD ELEVATION No. 7 TICKET COLLECTORS' ROOM

Chichester, Down Side

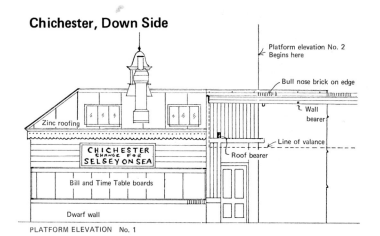

Platform elevation No. 2 Begins here

Bull nose brick on edge

Wall bearer

Line of valance

Zinc roofing

CHICHESTER
CHANGE FOR
SELSEY ON SEA

Roof bearer

Bill and Time Table boards

Dwarf wall

PLATFORM ELEVATION No. 1

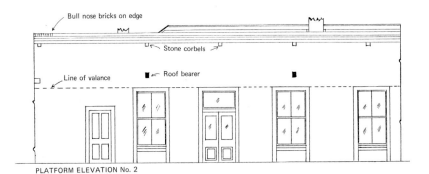

Bull nose bricks on edge

Stone corbels

Line of valance

Roof bearer

PLATFORM ELEVATION No. 2

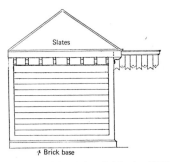

Slates

Brick base

END ELEVATION NO. 5   End elevation of Waiting room

Chichester, Down Side

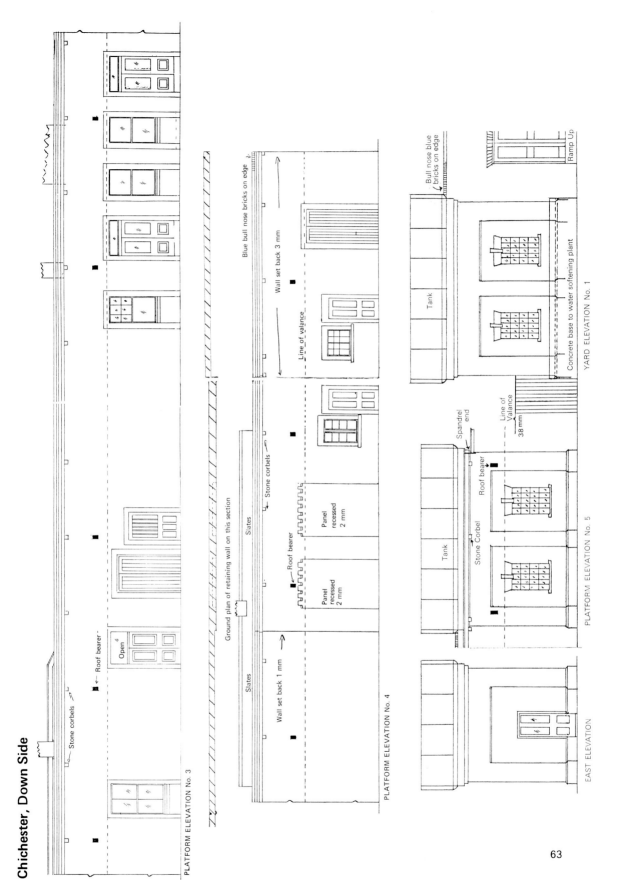

Stone corbels

Roof bearer

Open

PLATFORM ELEVATION No. 3

Ground plan of retaining wall on this section

Slates

Roof bearer

Stone corbels

Blue bull nose bricks on edge

Wall set back 3 mm

Line of valance

Wall set back 1 mm

Slates

Panel recessed 2 mm

Panel recessed 2 mm

PLATFORM ELEVATION No. 4

Bull nose blue bricks on edge

Tank

Concrete base to water softening plant

YARD ELEVATION No. 1

Spandrel end

Line of Valance 38 mm

Roof bearer

Tank

Stone Corbel

PLATFORM ELEVATION No. 5

EAST ELEVATION

Ramp Up

63

Chichester, Down Side

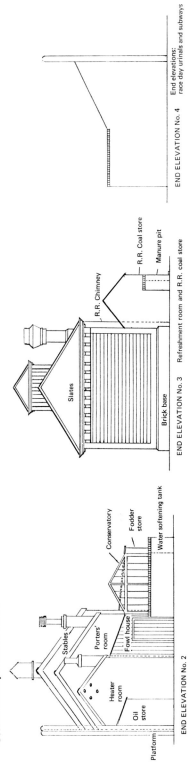

END ELEVATION No. 2

Platform

Oil store

Heater room

Fowl house

Porters' room

Stables

Conservatory

Fodder store

Water softening tank

END ELEVATION No. 3   Refreshment room and R.R. coal store

Slates

R.R. Chimney

R.R. Coal store

Manure pit

Brick base

END ELEVATION No. 4

End elevations: race day urinals and subways

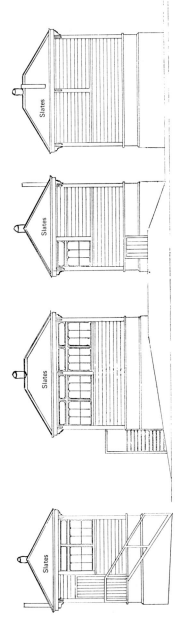

Slates

Slates

Slates

Slates

SIGNAL CABIN ON PLATFORM

Cottages at Chichester

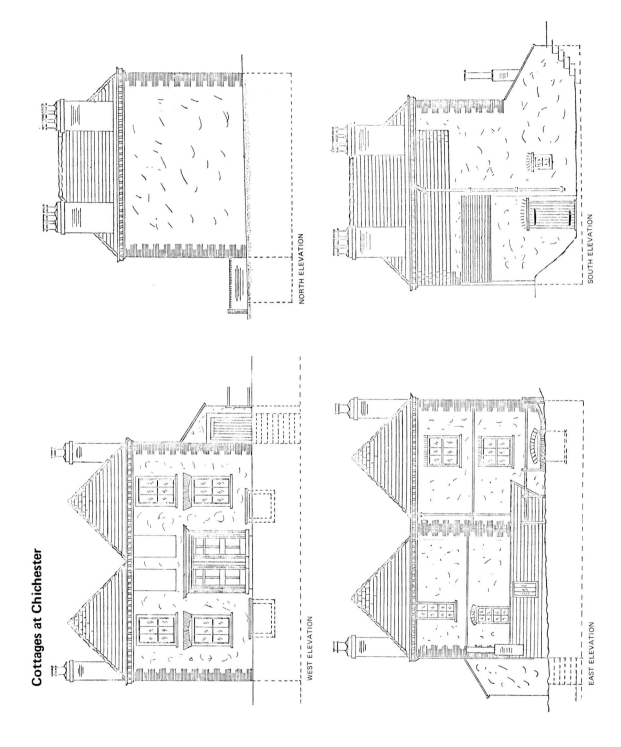

NORTH ELEVATION

SOUTH ELEVATION

WEST ELEVATION

EAST ELEVATION

65

Cottages at Chichester

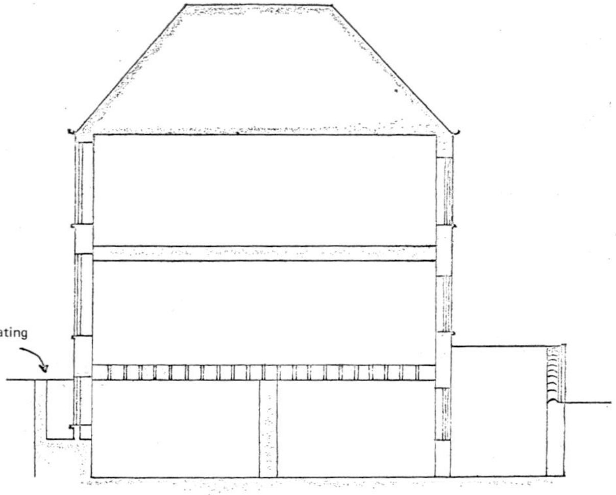
Iron grating

SECTION A – A

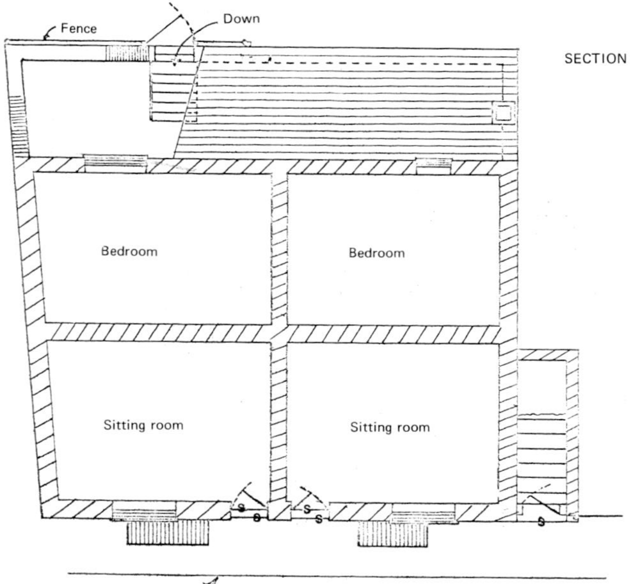
Fence
Down
Bedroom
Bedroom
Sitting room
Sitting room
S
S
S
S
S
Pavement

GROUND PLAN

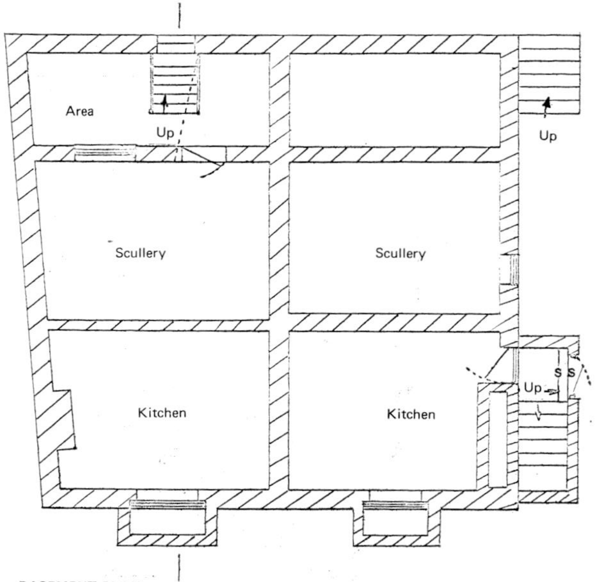
A
Area
Up
Up
Scullery
Scullery
Kitchen
Kitchen
S S
Up
A

BASEMENT PLAN

Chichester, Up Side

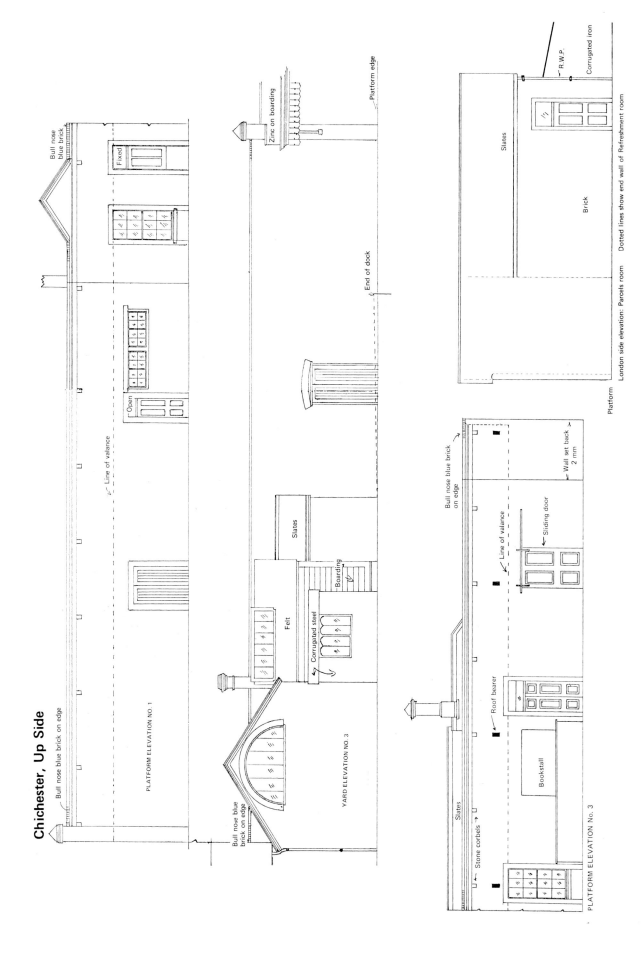

Bull nose blue brick

Bull nose blue brick on edge

Line of valance

PLATFORM ELEVATION NO. 1

Fixed

Open

Zinc on boarding

Platform edge

End of dock

Bull nose blue brick on edge

Slates

Felt

Boarding

Corrugated steel

YARD ELEVATION NO. 3

R.W.P.

Corrugated iron

Slates

Brick

Platform

London side elevation: Parcels room   Dotted lines show end wall of Refreshment room

Bull nose blue brick on edge

Line of valance

Sliding door

Wall set back 2 mm

Roof bearer

Slates

Stone corbels

Bookstall

PLATFORM ELEVATION NO. 3

Chichester, Up Side

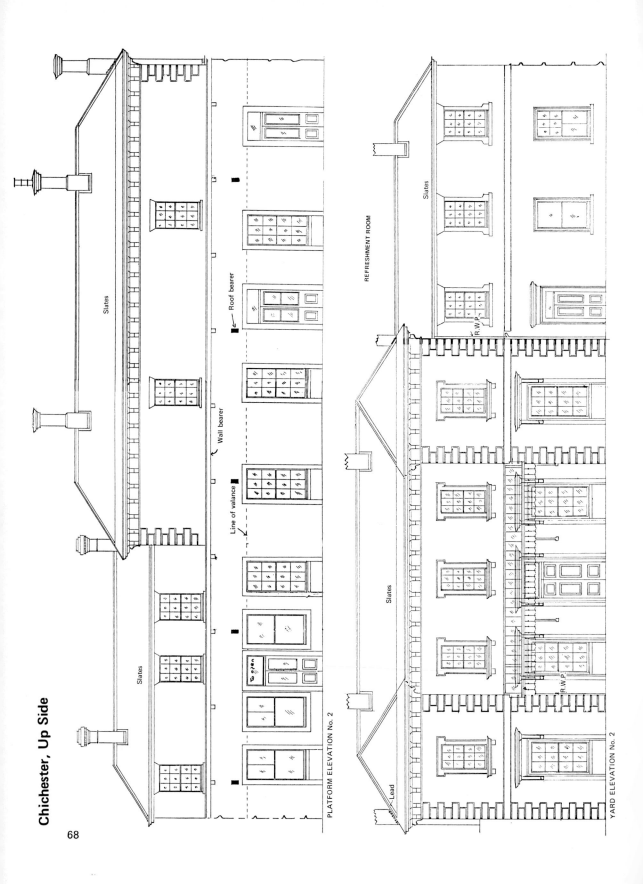

68

Slates

Slates

← Roof bearer

Wall bearer

Line of valance

PLATFORM ELEVATION No. 2

REFRESHMENT ROOM

Slates

Slates

R.W.P.

R.W.P.

Lead

YARD ELEVATION No. 2

Chichester, Up Side

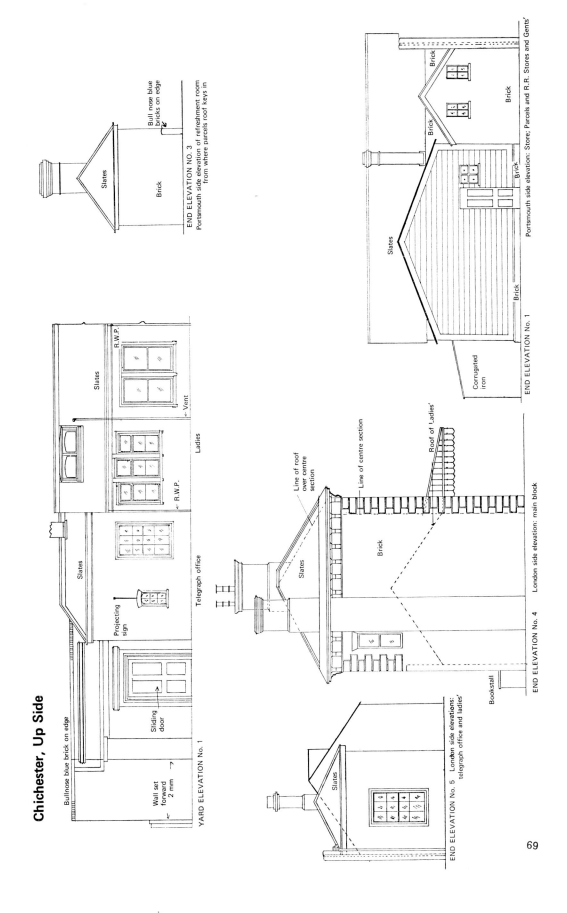

END ELEVATION NO. 3
Portsmouth side elevation of refreshment room
from where parcels roof keys in

Bull nose blue
bricks on edge

Slates

Brick

YARD ELEVATION No. 1

Bullnose blue brick on edge

Slates

Slates

R.W.P.

Vent

Ladies

R.W.P.

Telegraph office

Projecting
sign

Sliding
door

Wall set
forward
2 mm

Portsmouth side elevation: Store; Parcels and R.R. Stores and Gents'

Brick

Brick

Brick

Brick

Brick

Brick

Slates

Corrugated
iron

END ELEVATION No. 1

Line of roof
over centre
section

Line of centre
section

Roof of 'Ladies'

Slates

Brick

Bookstall

London side elevation: main block

END ELEVATION No. 4

Slates

END ELEVATION No. 5   London side elevations:
telegraph office and ladies'

69

Petworth

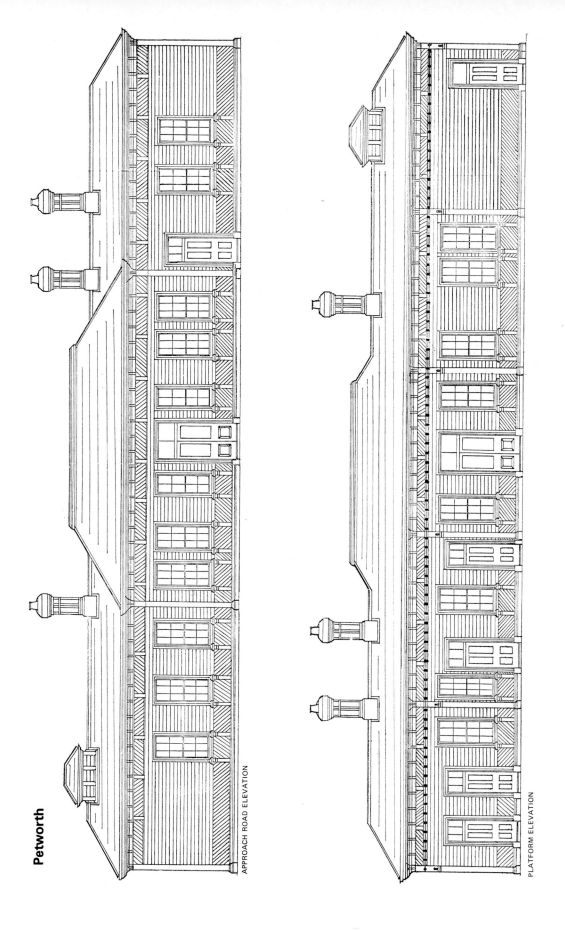

APPROACH ROAD ELEVATION

PLATFORM ELEVATION

Petworth

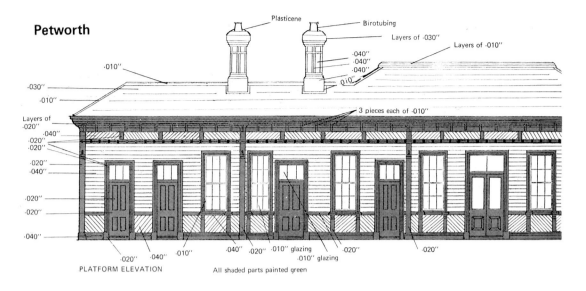

Plasticene
Birotubing
Layers of ·030"
Layers of ·010"
·040"
·040"
·040"
·010"
·010"
·030"
·010"
3 pieces each of ·010"
Layers of ·020"
·040"
·020"
·020"
·020"
·040"
·020"
·020"
·040"
·020" · ·040" · ·010" · ·040" · ·020" · ·010" glazing · ·010" glazing · ·020" · ·020"

PLATFORM ELEVATION

All shaded parts painted green

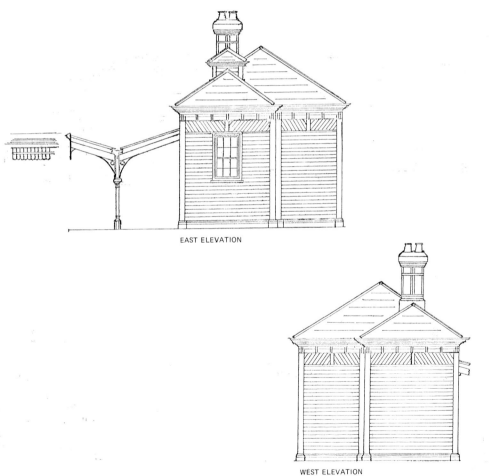

EAST ELEVATION

WEST ELEVATION

Fittleworth

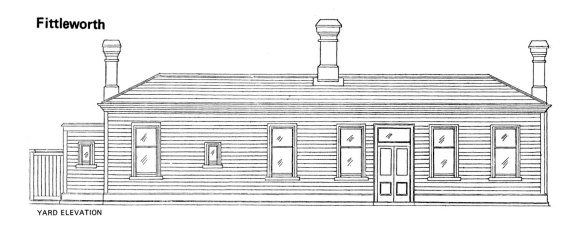

YARD ELEVATION

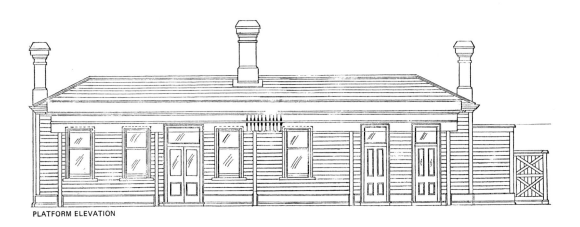

PLATFORM ELEVATION

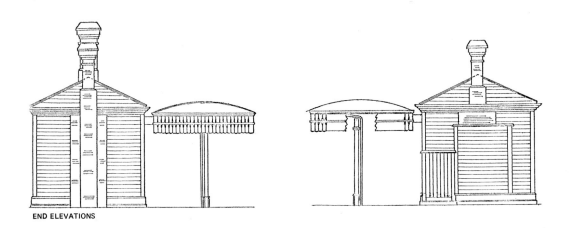

END ELEVATIONS

St. Leonards, West Marina

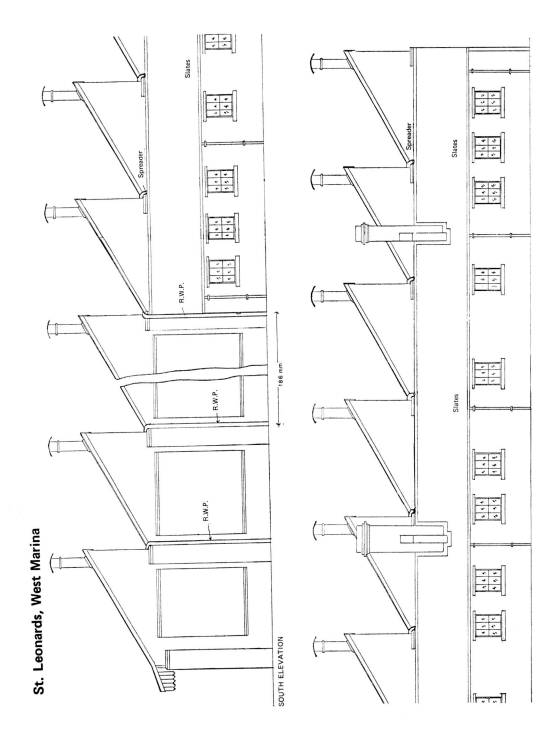

Slates

Spreader

R.W.P.

R.W.P.

R.W.P.

186 mm

Spreader

Slates

Slates

SOUTH ELEVATION

St. Leonards, West Marina — Loco Shed

EAST ELEVATION

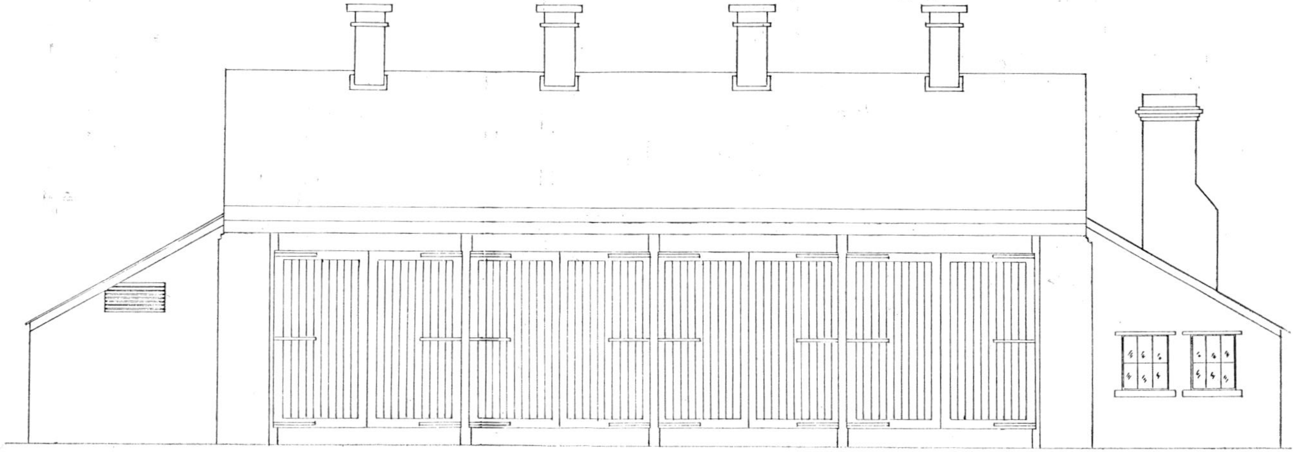

WEST ELEVATION

74

St. Leonards, West Marina,— Loco Shed

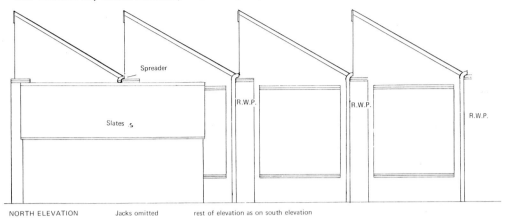

Spreader

Slates

R.W.P.

R.W.P.

R.W.P.

NORTH ELEVATION   Jacks omitted   rest of elevation as on south elevation

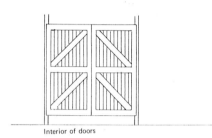

Interior of doors

Littlehampton, Signal Cabin

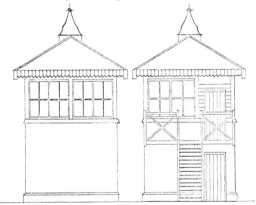

END ELEVATIONS

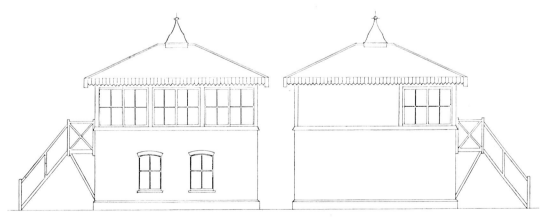

Littlehampton Station, Goods Warehouse

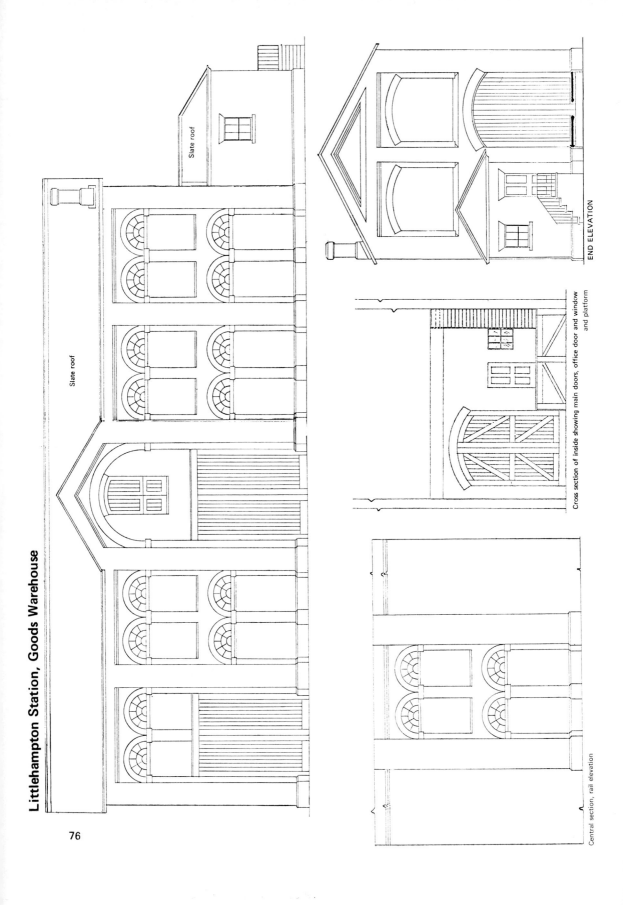

Slate roof

Slate roof

Central section, rail elevation

Cross section of inside showing main doors, office door and window and platform

END ELEVATION

Littlehampton, Loco Shed

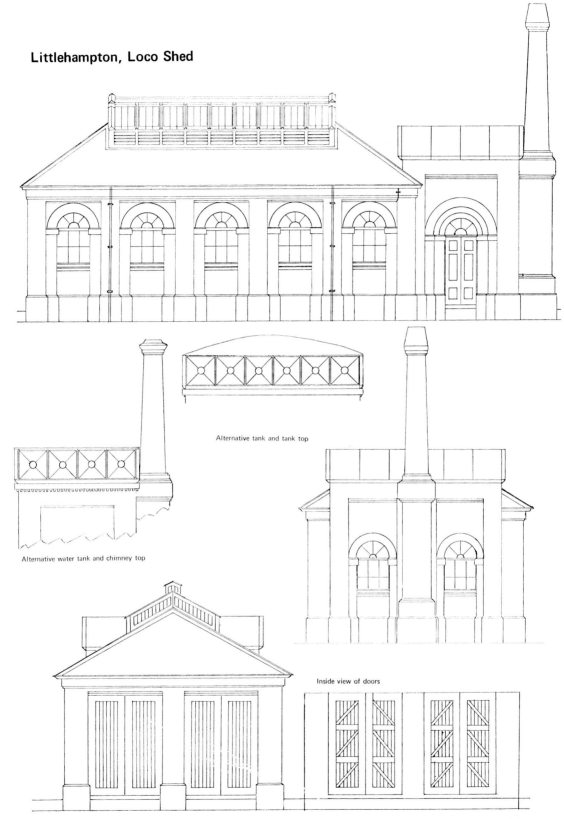

Alternative tank and tank top

Alternative water tank and chimney top

Inside view of doors

Pocklington

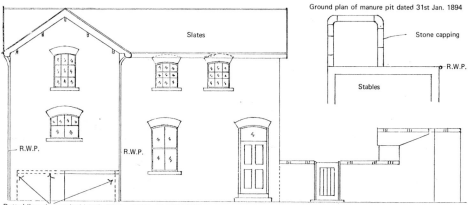

Ground plan of manure pit dated 31st Jan. 1894

Stone capping

R.W.P.

Stables

Slates

R.W.P.

R.W.P.

Dotted lines show revised length dated 7th Mar. 1894

SIDE ELEVATION

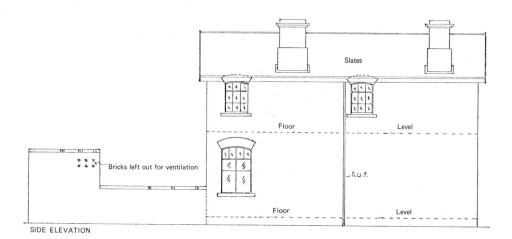

Slates

Floor   Level

Bricks left out for ventilation

R.W.?

Floor   Level

SIDE ELEVATION

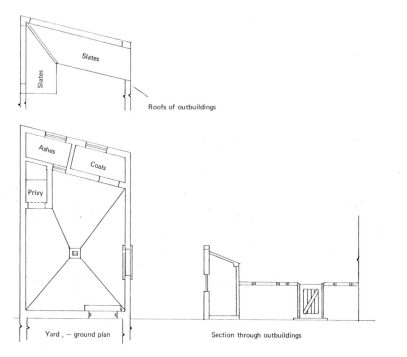

Slates

Slates

Roofs of outbuildings

Ashes

Coals

Privy

Yard , — ground plan

Section through outbuildings

Pocklington

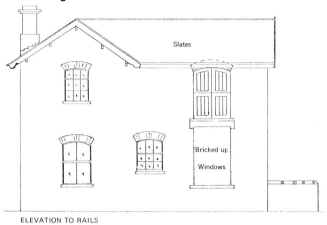

Slates

Bricked up
Windows

ELEVATION TO RAILS

Slates

Bricked up
windows

ELEVATION TO ROAD

2-2379